Peter Xu

林苑"双龙"译丛

总主编◎许景城

（汉英对照）

《弟子规》译介

——基于人类世生态诗学视角

[清] 李毓秀　[清] 贾存仁◎著

许景城◎译

[英] 瑞蒙·莫菲◎注并插画

Standards for Disciples

(Chinese and English)

An Anthropocenic

Ecopoetic Translation

Written by Yuxiu Li and Cunren Jia

Translated by Peter Jingcheng Xu

Illustrated by Raymond Murphy

We desperately need such eco-Confucian tonic at a challenging and worrisome time in the history of human relationships with the planet.

—Scott Slovic

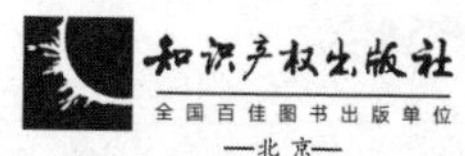

—北京—

图书在版编目（CIP）数据

《弟子规》译介：基于人类世生态诗学视角：汉英对照 /（清）李毓秀，（清）贾存仁著；许景城译．—北京：知识产权出版社，2020.7

ISBN 978-7-5130-6990-8

Ⅰ．①弟…　Ⅱ．①李…　②贾…　③许…　Ⅲ．①古汉语—启蒙读物—汉、英　②《弟子规》—注释　③《弟子规》—译文　Ⅳ．① H194.1

中国版本图书馆 CIP 数据核字 (2020) 第 099001 号

责任编辑：陈晶晶　　　　责任校对：谷　洋
封面设计：李志伟　　　　责任印制：刘译文

《弟子规》译介
——基于人类世生态诗学视角（汉英对照）

[清] 李毓秀　[清] 贾存仁　著　许景城　译
[英] 瑞蒙・莫菲　注并插画

出版发行：知识产权出版社有限责任公司　　网　　址：http：//www.ipph.cn
社　　址：北京市海淀区气象路 50 号院　　邮　　编：100081
责编电话：010-82000860 转 8391　　责编邮箱：shiny-chjj@163.com
发行电话：010-82000860 转 8101/8102　　发行传真：010-82000893/82005070/82000270
印　　刷：三河市国英印务有限公司　　经　　销：各大网上书店、新华书店及相关专业书店
开　　本：787mm×1092mm　1/32　　印　　张：9.5
版　　次：2020 年 7 月第 1 版　　印　　次：2020 年 7 月第 1 次印刷
字　　数：206 千字　　定　　价：59.00 元

ISBN 978-7-5130-6990-8

For the homes where I have studied, worked and dwelled

谨以此书献给我求学、工作和栖息的家园

This project is kindly sponsored by

Guangdong University of Foreign Studies

本书获广东外语外贸大学出版资助

Endorsements

Dr Peter Jingcheng Xu's Anthropocenic ecopoetic translation of *Dizigui* offers meaningful instructions for proper, mindful behaviour, showing that this classical Chinese text plays an important role in the tradition of world environmental literature. We desperately need such eco-Confucian tonic at a challenging and worrisome time in the history of human relationships with the planet.

—Scott Slovic, Professor of Literature and Environment at the University of Idaho, US

Dr Peter Jingcheng Xu's translation of *Dizigui* offers a timely take on an ancient text: it is a dialogical, a relational, and, in the end, a transcultural encounter between then and now, West and East, where connections can be sought and differences negotiated.

—Christopher Schliephake, Postdoctral Researcher of Cultural History and Ecocriticism at the University of Augsburg, Germany

推荐语

许景城博士从人类世生态诗学视角译介的《弟子规》，不仅为人类谨慎、正确的行为规范提供了有意义的借鉴，同时也展示了这部中国传统文化读本在世界环境文学史中所扮演的重要角色。如今，人类与地球关系史车轮正驶入危机四伏、忧心忡忡的时代，我们亟需这样一剂儒家生态的“警醒剂”。

——美国爱达荷大学文学与环境专业教授

斯科特·斯洛维克

许景城博士的英译本为典籍文本《弟子规》提供了符合时代的阐释：它彰显了对话性和关联性，最终，搭建了古今东西跨文化交流平台，展示了“追寻联结、商异求同”的可能性。

——德国奥格斯堡大学文化历史与生态批评博士后

研究员克里斯托弗·施利普哈克博士

As an overseas returnee and a young aficionado of English and Chinese literatures, Dr Peter Jingcheng Xu is credited with being adept at literary translation between English and Chinese. Xu's multimodal rendering of *Dizigui*, by multilayered, interactive and adroit means, introduces the Confucian primer to the world in pursuit of the smooth communication between China and foreign countries. How meritorious and beneficent it is!

—Professor Zhonglian Huang, Researcher of
the Center for Translation Studies,
Guangdong University of Foreign Studies

许景城博士系海归，英汉双语文青，英汉互译能手。其《弟子规》多模态译本以多元互动方式向世界巧妙地译介了儒家蒙学，旨在融通中外，功德无量。

——广东外语外贸大学翻译学研究中心专职研究员

黄忠廉教授

An Eco-Confucian Instruction Manual for Good Behaviour

Professor Scott Slovic

(University of Idaho, USA)

When I attempted to characterize the essential rhetorical elements of "nature writing" in a 1996 essay titled "Epistemology and Politics in American Nature Writing", I found myself dwelling on the vacillating proportions of "rhapsody" (celebratory language) and "jeremiad" (warning language) in literary prose concerned with the relationship between humans and the planet. Many writers I traced in my article, from Rachel Carson to Ann Zwinger, demonstrated variable mixtures of these modes of discourse. What I failed to discern in their writings, though, was the element of specific guidance or instruction, even though literary prose in Western culture, certainly in the American tradition, derives much of its heritage from the genre of the religious sermon, and sermons are inherently instructive. The sermonizer interprets a religious text and then uses this reading as the basis for guiding listeners toward right behaviour.

Henry David Thoreau came close to sermonizing in the "Higher Laws" chapter of *Walden* (1954), warning readers of the mind-numbing dangers of certain foods and drinks and advocating an ascetic diet he thought would support a "habit of attention", an awakened state of mind. Yet it is difficult to take anything at face value in *Walden*, as Thoreau's literary strategy was one of earnestly playful paradox and self-contradiction, one moment calling for the reading of ancient Greek and Latin texts as a way to keep one's mind alert, the next suggesting that the most noble thing to do is to hoe beans in the garden plot, and a few pages later expressing an animalistic yearning to devour a woodchuck raw. Just as it is difficult to decipher the moral prescriptions in *Walden*, I find it challenging to discern sermonic instructions in more recent environmental writing. Rachel Carson said we should beware of the dangers of agricultural pesticides in *Silent Spring* (1962), and Bill McKibben raised the clarion cry about global warming in *The End of Nature* (1989). Warnings—"Jeremiads"! Others, from Annie Dillard in *Teaching a Stone to Talk* (1982) to Rick Bass in *Wild to the Heart* (1987), celebrate the wildness of the human mind and the world beyond our control—— "Rapsody"! But both the jeremiadic and rhapsodic texts offer essentially the same broad instructions: "pay attention".

That's why it is somewhat startling, and curiously refreshing, for a Western reader to encounter *Dizigui*, this catalog of seven basic instructions, or "standards" of behaviour, regarding filial duties, brotherly behaviour, caution, honesty, love, goodness, and beauty. In his introduction to this volume, Peter Jingcheng Xu points to the Anthropocenic **urgency** of bringing together scholars from diverse disciplines, particularly from the sciences and the humanities, for "conversation about the endangered Earth in this bio-geological epoch of uncertainty". The sense of intensified urgency suggested here is also inspiring more and more trans-national collaborations and exchanges of cultural perspectives. This translation of *Dizigui* into English and its presentation together with multiple commentaries or artistic responses by the Chinese translator and various Western scholars exemplifies the spirit of international cooperation that characterizes what Xu calls "trans-cultural Anthropocenic ecopoetics". But there is a stark difference between the explicit didacticism in this book and what one typically finds in contemporary environmental humanities scholarship.

Recent scholarship excels at exploding our preconceptions about human relationships with the more-than-human and at revealing anthropogenic destruction of the planet and vulnerable human and non-human communities. Rob Nixon's *Slow Violence and the Environmentalism of the Poor* (2011) castigates neoliberal economic policy from an environmental justice and postcolonial ecocritical perspective, while Ursula Heise's *Imagining Extinction: The Cultural Meanings of Endangered Species* (2016) presents the ongoing disappearance of species as not only an ecological crisis but as a failure of the human imagination to appreciate (and react to) the magnitude of the crisis. A rising chorus of environmental scholars has reshaped our understanding of the human bond with physical nature: such publications as Stacy Alaimo's *Bodily Natures: Science, Environment, and the Material*

Self (2010) and Serenella Iovino and Serpil Oppermann's collection *Material Ecocriticism* (2014) highlights the constant flow "transcorporeal" of matter between human bodies and the body of the world and the inherent "story" within all physical phenomena. Sarah Nolan's *Unnatural Ecopoetics: Unlikely Spaces in Contemporary Poetry* (2017) operates with a broad and flexible view of "environment", including constructed spaces and even textual spaces within the rubric of ecopoetics, not only primal, organic territories and forces. In *Nature Writing of the Anthropocene* (2017), Christian Hummelsund Voie argues that Anthropocenic writing about the natural world must be fully attuned to the destructive impact of human action upon the planet's life-support systems and must therefore be almost exclusively jeremiadic in its condemnation of how our species behaves, how we **misbehave**. This is all important, consciousness-raising work, but it leaves readers without a blueprint for action.

Although the specific instructions available in *Dizigui* are mostly absent from Western environmental humanities scholarship, in a study titled *Affective Ecologies: Empathy, Emotion, and Environmental Narrative* (2017), Alexa Weik von Mossner cites Elaine Scarry's and Marco Caracciolo's theoretical work that compares literary narratives to "instruction manuals". Weik von Mossner takes the example of John Muir's classic text of American nature writing, *The Mountains of California* (1894), as a work that brings the reader through vivid narrative into the mountains and offers "instructions" through stories about how to properly experience the landscape and cherish the world. I would suggest that Xu's translation of *Dizigui* goes several steps further than Muir in offering specific instructions for proper, mindful behaviour. This eco-Confucian tonic is desperately needed at a time in history, the beginning of the third decade of the twenty-first century, when we worry not only about the chronic problems of human overpopulation, resource exploitation, and habitat despoilation, but the rogueish behaviour of regimes full of climate-change deniars, fossil-fuel executives, hyper-nationalists, and xenophobes.

Moscow, Idaho

16/01/2018

A Transcultural Poetics

Dr Christopher Schliephake

(University of Augsburg, Germany)

One of the powerful effects of this work by Peter Jingcheng Xu is that it makes one meditate on the processes involved in what I want to call a "transcultural poetics". To be sure, we have not yet overcome dualisms between West and East, or discursive formations connected to these fated words (as shown by Foucault, Said and others). And as a reader with a cultural background connected to the humanistic traditions of Western learning, there is an inherent danger to fall back on Orientalist images when dealing with Chinese culture, to project one's own cultural stereotypes into the text, to irrevocably compare a foreign culture to one's own. In general, there is nothing inherently wrong with that — after all, one of the effects of a liberal education is the attempt to understand worlds (and words) far removed from our own, indeed to project oneself partway into otherness. But there is a crucial double bind involved, because the engagement with the other means that one's own cultural identity comes to the fore and the hermeneutic process implied in reading a text can turn into an exercise in negotiating one's own beliefs, passions, and values.

The triad between Chinese original, English poetic translation, and interpretative version as offered in this volume is an ingenious way of epitomizing the different levels involved in translation processes. Etymologically, translation means "carried over" (from Latin "transferre"). It is a process not only of turning something from one language to another, but also of removing something from one place and moving it to another one. This is exactly what is happening in this book: chronologically, it reaches from the poetic deep-layers of China's infinitely rich cultural history to our own day and age, while it covers whole continents in its spatial outlook. To most European (or Western) readers, the original three-character poems will remain a closed book; with our 26-letter Latin alphabet, we can only marvel at the craft included in writing and deciphering the Chinese script — "to marvel" is indeed a freighted term, often connected to aesthetic experience or to the encounter with the "exotic". I refer to it in the first sense, because the beautiful artwork of the volume hints at the multiple levels of meaning involved in the different sections, resonating with the images evoked by poetic language and the thematic coherence of the individual texts. That Xu chose to offer a prose translation along with a poetic one is a decision that needs to be applauded; the more so, as it uncovers the difficulties involved in conveying the meaning of the Chinese three-character poems in another language. However, it is especially Xu's own poetic translation of the source text that shows how he grapples with a foreign language himself, how he becomes attentive to its nuances and their cultural contexts in the twenty-first century. This makes this book a dialogical, a relational, and, in the end, a transcultural undertaking, where connections can be sought and differences negotiated. It is my belief that the dualism between East and West still prevalent in the media and cultural projections is in need of some reformulation and that transculturalism is one way of bridging the differences in-between. To be sure, that does not mean that differences should be negated, quite the contrary. It just means that culture itself should no longer appear as a static container of nationalist self-representation, but rather as a fluid and permeable space for encounter where new forms of communication, co-existence, and collaboration can be sought. A transcultural poetics, then, is a connecting link between times and places, aesthetic forms of expression and their readers. It shows how the poetic knowledge of another time or another country can reach out and touch us.

Why is this important? On the one hand, there is an increasing trend of perceiving history as world history. By this, I do not only refer to the "transnational turn" that is currently re-shaping some of our common frameworks or that wants to comment on our condition in a globalized age. But also to so many cultural texts that reframe history in its global (as opposed to local) dimensions: as Michael Scott in the BBC documentary series "Ancient Worlds", now also available as a book (London: Hutchinson, 2016), Peter Frankopan (*The Silk Roads: A New History of the*

World, London: Bloomsbury, 2016) and others have shown, there are age-old connecting links between and across civilizations and geographical spaces that have not only been important for economic and sociopolitical (or geopolitical) processes, but that have shaped ideas and imaginations. These manifold intersections and interactions have often been overlooked and forgotten (for instance, in Eurocentric conceptualizations of history), but they have nevertheless existed. Highlighting connection is not the same as arguing for globalization or unification — quite the contrary. And this is also an aspect that a transcultural poetics can bring to the fore: there are important differences in aesthetic representation and limits of understanding, but there are also ways of communicating across these differences and of finding out where common points of reference lie. The high degree of discipline and respect as well as other rules of conduct emphasized in *Dizigui* may strike European readers as odd, or even outdated, but we should not forget that our own literary history is full of examples that reflected on right and respectful behaviour (Homer's epics were an exercise in right behaviour for his readers/listeners in antiquity). Every civilization has its distinct characteristics and treasures that need to be valued and that should not be made the object of un-reflected adaption (or hegemonic erasure) by another one — especially in a highly commodified and digitalized age. A transcultural poetics as offered in this book can uncover the productive space marked by both connectivity and difference from which new forms of co-existence and understanding can be sought. This entails an engagement with Chinese philosophy and pedagogy by Europeans, as well as, for instance, a reflection on cultural values in European theories of democracy by the Chinese. Not the "either/or" but the "both/and" are highlighted in a transcultural reading of cultural interaction.

The second reason is tied to this socio-historical or — political dimension, but it transcends the level of interpersonal anthropocentrism. As Dipesh Chakrabarty, Ursula Heise and others have noted, we have entered a period in the history of our species, where we are often painfully reminded of the fragility of our global ecosystem. The ecological crisis, which shows itself not only in extreme weather events, climate change and the like, but also in human-made risk scenarios through toxic pollution or atomic energy, is not restrained to local boundaries, but rather a global phenomenon. And because it is a global phenomenon that concerns us all and demands new models of cooperation and co-existence between communities, political institutions, and the non-human, new ways of imagining ecological interrelations are called for. I would argue that they are necessarily transcultural, not only because they deal with the same phenomena, but also because the confrontation with unprecedented risk scenarios and scales brings forth new ways of communicating about and dealing with global issues. Again, there will be differences in more way than one, but the connective aspects are at least equally important. With the stanza, "Man in feeling/love every being./Same Heaven share; same Earth bear", Yuxiu Li and Cunren Jia enter the debate and offer a cosmopolitan viewpoint that, despite cultural meanings of which I am sure there are a lot that elude me, strikes home a powerful message. Indeed, rules of conduct and right behaviour go hand in hand with coming to grips with an ecological crisis: waste removal, recycling, use of public transit, etc. — all of these aspects demand individual action and responsibility. They are especially called for in high-density habitats like urban environments. Architects, urban planners, and social scientists have long begun to think about place-based solutions to ecological problems. The Biennale Architecture 2016 in Venice, curated by Chilean architect Alejandro Aravena, and published in a beautiful two-volume book (*Reporting From the Front*, Venice: Marsilio 2016) is a good example of how national approaches to urban ecology come together in a shared space of ideas. The language and images employed in this exhibition are clearly transcultural, often focusing on processes of migration, movement, mobility. What made clear is that the public need to be engaged with, as much as the political planners and leaders are called on to integrate their top-down designs in community-based frameworks, where bottom-up initiatives will likewise be possible. We all, for better or worse, make and re-make our environments on a daily basis. Even if we choose not to follow every advice or rule found in *Dizigui*, the book is a helpful reminder that we are integrated in complex networks of interaction. Texts and translations are an invaluable resource in shaping how we see our planet. It is my hope that what we, as humanists, can add to the bigger picture of these global entanglements is a transcultural imagination.

Augsburg

06/10/2016

Eco-Affinities between *Dizigui* and Environmental Western Campaigners

Professor Ian Gregson

(Bangor University, Wales, UK)

There is an important affinity between the values of *Dizigui* and those which environmental campaigners such as Naomi Klein are promoting as vital for the survival of the planet. Peter Jingcheng Xu describes the text as "a significant guide book for individuals of our age to better and purify their selves, and cultivate and enhance their ecological sensibilities that underpin family, social and environmental duties". The difference in vocabulary should not disguise the connection with Klein's stress on collective values: she sees in the prospect of environmental disaster cause for a paradoxical hope that the crisis will be understood as so severe that it demands a thorough transformation of the capitalist values that have placed the planet in such danger.

She insists that the acute sense of impending disaster will lead to a move away from individualistic appetite towards a new collective spirit and forms of community action which are required to address the effects of environmental change and to moderate their impact, and which will, in that process, transform politics.[①]

Such environmental campaigning has arisen against the grain of the postmodernist sensibility which became so influential in the 1950s onwards: postmodernism is urban and metropolitan. The New York poet Frank O'Hara said that he was never comfortable unless there was a subway handy[②], and this camp anti-nature stance is characteristically postmodern, much more thoroughly citified than the sensibility behind T.S. Eliot's *The Waste Land* with its montaged urban/natural contrasts. Eliot's satire arises out of his horror at the unnaturalness of modern culture, but in the postmodern this unnaturalness has intensified and established itself as a norm. For Fredric Jameson,

---

① KLEIN N. This Changes Everything: Capitalism vs. the Climate [M]. London: Penguin, 2014.

② O'HARA F. Meditations in an Emergency [C]. // The Collected Poems of Frank O'Hara. New York: Knopf, 1979: 197.

the superseding of nature is a defining characteristic of postmodernism, which is the condition that is reached "when the modernization process is complete and nature is gone for good"①.

Writers, like Jameson, with Marxist leanings tended until recently to express ambiguous responses to this process. Walter Benjamin② analyses the reifications involved but also sees in the culture of mechanical reproduction the possibilities of a transformative politics which might lead to new, post-capitalist identities. Donna J. Haraway's half-ironic praise for cyborgs is similarly optimistic about the potential of the changed selves that technology might bring. She opposes the organicism of radical feminists such as Susan Griffin, Audré Lourd and Adrienne Rich, with their "eco-feminism and feminist paganism", with a celebration of the ontological potential of late twentieth-century machines which call into question the boundaries between the organic and the mechanical,

① JAMESON F. Postmodernism or, the Cultural Logic of Late Capitalism [M]. London: Verso, 1991: ix.

② BENJAMIN W. The Work of Art in the Age of Mechanical Reproduction [C]. // Illuminations. London: Pimlico, 1999.

because they "have made thoroughly ambiguous the difference between natural and artificial, mind and body, self-developing and externally designed, and many other distinctions that used to apply to organisms and machines. Our machines are disturbingly lively, and we ourselves frighteningly inert"①.

By contrast, Teresa Brennan connects the superseding of nature to the activities of a consumer capitalism which is so destructive that it produces a culture which is mentally ill:

> if nature is endlessly consumed in the pursuit of a totalizing course, then the course is dangerous for living; it constitutes a danger to one's own survival, as well as that of others. That, approximately, is the technical, legal definition of psychosis.②

In her later work, the postcolonial theorist Gayatri Spivak expresses similar anxieties to those theorised by

---

① HARAWAY D J. Simians, Cyborgs, and Women: a Cyborg Manifesto [C]. // Simians, Cyborgs, and Women: The Reinvention of Nature. London: Free Association Books, 1991:174.

② BRENNAN T. History after Lacan [M]. London and New York: Routledge, 1993: 4.

Teresa Brennan. At the start of her career, Spivak became famous as a translator and interpreter of the work of Jacques Derrida, so her ecological turn represents a break with her earlier link to postmodernist theorising. It is true that, even from early on, Spivak's postcolonial and gender concerns politicised her attitude to deconstruction. Nonetheless, she was noted above all for her scepticism about the possibility of effective political action, given the thoroughly oppressive power with which Western hegemonic structures have been imposed on colonial peoples. For her, the extent to which "subaltern" peoples can speak is inevitably thoroughly limited.

Those attitudes have undergone a subtle but tellingly representative shift in Spivak's work. There is a starkly unpostmodernist earnestness, for example, in the language of her "Afterword" of her translation of the stories of the Bengali writer and political activist Mahasweti Devi.① Her idiom there is the opposite of that wearily sophisticated irony employed by Fredric Jameson — as too is the content.

① LANDRY D, MACLEAN G. The Spivak Reader [M]. New York: Routledge, 1996: 267-286.

Far from believing that nature can be eschewed, Spivak is distraught at the damage inflicted upon it by the West's Enlightenment rationality and looks to oppose that destructiveness with an emphasis on ethical responsibility and — most remarkable of all — "love". Her point is that the threat to global ecology is so great that an almost hopeless undertaking is required, combining the efforts of previously irreconcilable forces — "the silent gift of the subaltern" (the impossible but still necessary struggle of suppressed colonial people) and an Enlightenment reason reoriented so that its impact is genuinely rational.

It is these attitudes which come closest, in Western thought, to the values of *Dizigui* — this spirit of rigorous "love" propounded by Spivak, and the collective values and the spirit of community, stressed by Naomi Klein. These attitudes have always been key aspects, also of Welsh culture and are repeatedly invoked by Welsh poets such as John Barnie and Robert Minhinnick. Minhinnick's extended critique of consumerism in postindustrial Wales is part of the way his work takes Wales as the starting-point of a global politics focusing on colonialism and nature.

His sympathy for native peoples is not sentimental because it is part of a much larger environmentalist vision. He has talked about his poem "Ants" in these terms, saying that it "is about Australia, the arrogance of power, and the disinherited. In the US I've worked with native people who felt instinctively that uranium mining was destroying their sacred places. But 'Ants' was influenced by proposals for opencasting of coal in Welsh landscapes. Opencasting destroys everything from geology to field names. It creates a kind of amnesia, which is one of the processes by which the sacred is lost from life"[①].

So a profound malaise is evoked in his poem "The Hot-House"[②] by the interpenetration of the natural and the queasily unnatural, and the pervasive sense of the one sickening into the other. The stems of nettles are as hollow "as hypodermics" elderberries fade into "dull newsprint". The hot-house is an artificial rainforest but it reflects what

---

① GREGSON I. On the Street of Processions: an Interview with Robert Minhinnick [J]. Planet, 2004, 167 (10): 47.

② MINHINNICK R. Selected Poems [M]. Manchester: Carcanet, 1999: 94-100.

is happening in actual rainforests with a clock that registers forest acres lost every second, and with a leaflet that "tells of species that become extinct before they are discovered".

Minhinnick stresses, as *Dizigui* does, the vital need for stabilities and traditional forms of respect. In "Twenty-Five Laments for Iraq"[①], his poem about the war in Iraq, the destruction of nature is invoked in precisely these terms — the animals in the poem (wolves, desert birds, a kingfisher, bats, lizards and a heron) are all invoked living on the ignored margins of the human conflict, but their presence hints at an alternative system of values and an implied rebuke that becomes explicit when they build to a reference to the Uranium spilled at Ur, and the four billion years it will take to render it safe. For Minhinnick, the mingling of the natural and the unnatural is symptomatic; the atrocities reveal that the horrors committed in state politics and those committed in ecological politics are indistinguishable from each other. The vision that shapes these poems, therefore,

---

① MINHINNICK R. After the Hurricane [M]. Manchester: Carcanet, 2002: 7-11.

with its ecological stress on the connection between the individual and the collective, has a remarkable affinity with that of *Dizigui*.

Bangor, Wales

25/02/2018

An Anthropocenic Ecopoetics: the Case of *Dizigui*

Dr Peter Jingcheng Xu

(Guangdong University of Foreign Studies, China; Bangor University, Wales, UK)

We are now entering the era of the Anthropocene, which literally means the "Age of Man", signalling that humanity has become a geological force and an agent in transforming our planet.① Humanity is even for the first time being considered by biologists as the likely culprit for the sixth massive extinction event in history.② The Earth, since the 1960s, has encountered escalating ecological challenges and disasters with ramifications for the ecosystem: melting

① CRUTZEN P. Geology of Mankind [J]. Nature, 2002, 415(6867): 23.

② HEISE U. Imagining Extinction: The Cultural Meanings of Endangered Species [M]. Chicago: University of Chicago Press, 2016.

polar glaciers, global warming, irregular tsunamis, ozone layer depletion, acid rain, the increasing extinction of species, exponentially increasing population, oil spills in the Pacific Ocean, deforestation, desertification, irregular earthquakes and hurricanes, volcano eruptions, and the nuclear reactor catastrophes in Chernobyl and Fukushima. The planet we are inhabiting has experienced unprecedented ecological crises. "If current trends continue," Daniel Maguire reminds us, "we will not. And this is qualitatively and epochally true"①. A recent "Editorial" of *English* highlights that, in our era of pressing environmental challenges, we need to find answers urgently, "What matters more now than asking the question how we can improve the terms of our relationship with the environment? We need answers because the problems caused by our current relationship are stark"②. Such answers must be connected to the way that humans perceive themselves and their place in the world. Thus, although natural science is credited

① MAGUIRE D. The Moral Core of Judaism and Christianity: Reclaiming the Revolution [M]. Philadelphia: Fortress Press, 1993: 13.

② The English Editorial Team. Editorial [J]. English, 2016, 65(251): 291.

with pinpointing environmental problems and searching for tentative scientific solutions, our unprecedented ecological predicament cannot be fully surmounted without the environmental humanities.

This epoch entails a more urgent need than any other in history for inter/transdisciplinary engagement, dialogue, and cooperation between the environmental sciences and the humanities. Serpil Oppermann and Serenella Iovino articulate this need to "bring the social sciences, the humanities, and the natural sciences together in diverse ways to address the current ecological crises from closely knit ethical, cultural, philosophical, political, social, and biological perspectives"①.

The "Anthropocenic turn" in scholarship thus brings critics with different backgrounds into conversation about the endangered Earth in this bio-geological epoch of uncertainty. This is crucial, since scientific knowledge and solutions, though valuable, are no longer good enough in

---

① OPPERMANN S, IOVINO S. Introduction: The Environmental Humanities and the Challenges of the Anthropocene [C] // OPPERMANN S, IOVINO S. ed. Environmental Humanities: Voices from the Anthropocene. London: Rowman & Littlefield International, 2016: 1.

isolation, as Paddy Woodworth underlines:

> Scientific knowledge is vital but on its own will never change our environmental behaviour. The key to that is to incorporate skills from the other side of the traditional science-humanities divide.[①]

The necessity of resorting to traditional humanities disciplines is also expressly stressed by James Gustave Speth: "Our environmental discourse has thus far been dominated by lawyers, scientists, and economists. Now, we need to hear a lot more from the poets, preachers, philosophers, and psychologists."[②] Thus, the current ecological discourse should be widely inclusive, reaching out to plumb the humanities for ecological solutions. It needs more dialogues and cooperation between East and West. In this context, I coin the term "Anthropocenic Ecopoetics" which encourages a cross-cultural dialogue,

---

① WOODWORTH P. The Art of Changing the Climate Debate [J/OL]. The Irish Times (2016-06-11) [2016-09-28]. http://www.irishtimes.com/news/environment/the-art-of-changing-the-climate-debate-1.2675671.

② SPETH J G. Angels by the River: a Memoir [M]. Vermont: Chelsea Green Publishing, 2014: 157.

cooperation and rapport between East and West in addressing the disconcerting climate change in the Anthropocene by means of transforming and refining humanity from within, enlightened by ecological wisdoms found in traditional and modern Humanities, with a shared ultimate goal of establishing an inhabitable, sustainable, peaceful, and harmonious Earth. To this end, we need to relinquish bias and stereotypes in their various disguise, and dismantle the East-West dualism, when dealing with different and foreign humanities, just as Shliephake's preface reminds us. On China's side, what is the use or good of traditional Chinese humanities in the face of the depleting Earth? What answers can they offer? Prompted by the severity of environmental quandaries and the width and depth of human impact, and responding to the call for contribution and cooperation by the humanities, I have become aware of the importance and imperativeness of revisiting, translating, and interpreting some Chinese classics, like *Daodejing*, *The Analects of Confucius* and *Dizigui*, in hopes that they can lend some plausible remedies to appalling ecological realities and encourage a transformation and refinement of humanity, in an attempt to initiate, across cultures, dialogues that will pluralize and enrich the current Western ecopoetic discourses.

The term "ecopoetics" was coined by Jonathan Bate in his monograph *The Song of the Earth* (2000). For Bate, "ecopoetics" as an ecological criticism is more phenomenological than "ecocriticism". As he observes, the essential objective of environmental criticism should not be "a form of political criticism in the manner of feminism and post-colonialism", albeit he also admits that ecocriticism can make contributions to green politics.① Rather, it should be more "phenomenological than political"②. By "phenomenological", Bate means that "ecopoetics" describes the outside world through verse, showing its humanistic concerns towards deteriorating environmental realities rather than taking the form of political activism like environmentalist movements.③ He attempts to justify his position by reverting to etymology: "eco" comes from the Greek "oikos", meaning "the home or place of dwelling"; "critic" stems from "kritis", meaning "judge"; and "poetics" derives from "poiesis", meaning "verse making".

---

① BATE J. The Song of the Earth [M]. Cambridge, Massachusetts: Harvard University Press, 2002: 75.

② Ibid.

③ Ibid: 75-76.

For Bate, "ecopoetics" concerns in what aspects poetry can be "the making of a dwelling place"[①]. In this sense, Bate does not simply identify poetry with verse, but also believes that the techniques of verse-making would be good methods to underwrite the making of a dwelling place: "the rhythmic, syntactic and linguistic intensifications that are characteristic of verse making frequently give a peculiar force to the poiesis" and "meter itself — a quiet but persistent music, a recurring cycle, a heartbeat — is an answering to nature's own rhythms, an echoing of the song of the earth itself ".[②] Thus, as Bate claims, "poiesis in the sense of verse-making is language's most direct path of return to the oikios"[③]. William Howarth suggests that "oikos" means nature, "our widest home" and "kritis" means "an arbiter who wants to keep the house in good order"[④]. As Bate observes, Howarth's understanding of "kritis" indicates a green political proclivity: how to well maintain the

---

① BATE J. The Song of the Earth [M]. Cambridge, Massachusetts: Harvard University Press, 2002: 75.

② Ibid: 75-76.

③ Ibid: 76.

④ HOWARTH William. Ecocriticism in Context [C] // COUPE L. Ed. The Green Studies Reader: from Romanticism to Ecocriticism. London and New York: Routledge, 2000: 163.

earth, our house in good condition is the responsibility that ecocritics as arbiters should shoulder. Gifford does not agree on this point because Bate, in his perception, still sticks to the outdated separation of poetry and politics.① Thus, he maintains that poetry still has an important role in making "a shift in sensibility rather than life-style"②. I side with Bate in the argument that ecopoetics should be principally oriented towards literature and phenomenology. That's why when translating this Confucian literature, I exert all possible efforts to maintain the formal equivalence and faithfulness to the original texts (which will be detailed in later sections) in hopes that the original poetic aesthetics and ideorealm can be conveyed to target-language readers, and engage a dynamic dialogue and inter-reference with other literatures, like Welsh literature, Welsh writing in English, English-language literature, to name but a few. For this concern, I invite Emeritus Professor Ian Gregson as a highly-established and award-winning British poet from the School of English Literature, Bangor University,

① GIFFORD T. Green Voices: Understanding Contemporary Nature Poetry [M]. 2nd ed. Nottingham: Critical, Cultural and Communications Press, 2011: 8.

② Ibid.

to curate the preface that unravels the literary exchange and some unexpected eco-poetic and aesthetic affinities between *Dizigui* and Western literatures.

Admittedly, Bates' framework of "literary-oriented" ecopoetics, albeit functionally important, is slightly narrow in scope. For this reason, I equally concur with Gifford's afore-mentioned proposal on the grounds that poetry does not simply depict literary phenomena but also weaves poets' political views in reference to their surrounding environment. In other words, "ecopoetics" unavoidably displays its political and social orientation, not least because ecological visions emanating from literary texts are highly relevant to our Anthropocenic reality, offering us some ecologically harmonious and holistic thinking patterns to rewrite our current lifestyle and governing environmental policies defined by strong anthropocentricism as a root cause of ecological crises. It is evident that Bate, actually conscious of the flaw of his literary ecopoetic framework, feels it impossible to totally exclude political concerns: the focus of ecopoetics will be diverted from phenomenological to political, when literary works concern gender, race, and power.[1] A political-oriented definition is not contradictory to a literary-oriented one. Rather, they are mutually complementary. To extend this further, I argue that ecopoetics aims to examine literary (and even multi-modal) texts that not only imaginatively and phenomenologically represent realities and environments but also convey prospective philosophical, political, educational, social and ecological values which transcend different nations and cultures, showing a great potential of becoming universal values (this trajectory, as I see it, is an important concern, marker and criterion for World Literature) characterized by holistic thinking that is conducive to bettering humanity and protecting natural and anthropogenic environments, and re-establishing a harmonious homeland of our Earth.

The redefinition of ecopoetics that underpins the trajectory from one culture to another raises an unavoidable question concerning how the term "translation" is reflected in this article. As Homi K. Bhabha defines, translation is not confined to textual and linguistic senses alone, but

① BATE J. The Song of the Earth [M]. Cambridge, Massachusetts: Harvard University Press, 2002: 76.

extended to in Sussan Bassnet's words "the etymological sense of being carried from one place to another"①. In the same vein, I regard "translation" as a process of decoding texts from one language to another. My English deciphering of this Chinese-language Confucian text surely falls into this category. Meanwhile, I emphasize "translation" more as a vital dynamic trajectory of "bringing" or "transferring" Eastern cultural texts to Western academia, and vice versa, in pursuit of the equal, vibrant and non-hegemonic dialogues between East and West. It is hoped that this ecopoetic translation will not leave readers, especially those engaged in post-colonist studies, an impression that it involves a new cultural postcolonism like Bhabha's sense of translation usually incurs. In this sense, it echoes the original meaning of the term "translation" as "carried over" (from "transferre" in Latin) without a tint of colonialism, as Christopher's preface etymologically traces. Additionally, I also consider "translation" involves the process either of "applying" theories (like ecocriticism) as

---

① BASSNETT S. Translation Studies[M]. 3rd ed. London: Routledge, 2002: 6.

outer forces to texts and discourses as inner forces in order to manifest certain thoughts conveyed in the discourses, or of "deciphering" thoughts conveyed in texts to enrich or challenge current theories, and then of transferring them from one region to another in a faithful manner or in well-intentioned alteration. In this respect, it is reminiscent of how Christopher in his preface underwrites "translation" as a process of "removing something from one place and moving it to another one". Premised on the aforementioned argument, it sounds reasonable that translation of ecopoetic critiques of the Anthropocene is a cross-literary and trans-cultural activity behind inter-linguistic decoding. With this in mind, readers will better understand my intent to invite and arrange a consortium of leading critics with different knowledge and national backgrounds to engage in the areas that can, to varying degrees, demonstrate their particular expertise to translate *Dizigui*. It is also true of Ray Murphy's multimodal translation by painting the illustrations and composing his own ekphrastic poems alongside them so that readers can approach and imagine in multifarious ways those Confucian guidelines mentioned in this book. Noted that this arrangement can also be considered as an attempt to aggrandize the academic value of certain texts like *Dizigui* and their potential of being enshrined as world literature, in the context of the increasing international popularity and dissemination of Chinese culture and literature.

The trans-cultural Anthropocenic ecopoetics actually speaks itself to the "Belt and Road Initiative", proposed by President Xi Jinping, which promotes international cooperation in tackling global ecological challenges, as well as economic cooperation between China and the countries along the "Silk Road Economic Belt" and the "Maritime Silk Road". Such developments are encouraging, and unfortunately they must be set against some regressive steps in Western countries, not least those of the tycoon and isolationist Donald Trump. As we have already seen, the current leader of the Western world not only sacrifices global cooperation with his America-first policies, but also denies the realities of environmental depletion and on 1 June, 2017 shamelessly announced a US withdrawal from the Paris climate change agreement. As is underlined by this American hindering of global environmental protection, criticisms of China's environmental credentials are unbalanced at best. As China has now realized, addressing ecological issues entails robust, publicized schemes of modern environmental management and protection.① But it also entails paying more attention to traditional bodies of thoughts, including Daoism and Confucianism. As Chinese President Xi Jinping has mentioned, these bodies

---

① The changing attitude of the Chinese central government, towards curbing uncontrolled economic development and implementing environmental protection, can be evidenced. For example, by the central government granting permission for the release, in early March 2015, of the alarming documentary of the well-known CCTV journalist Chai Jing. The documentary concerns China's deteriorating environmental situation, with Chai advocating increased public awareness of ecological protection and a more harmonious economic development model. The determination of the Chinese Central Government to address serious environmental problems can be further evidenced by an announcement of the Fifth Plenary Session of the 18th Party Congress, on 27th October 2015. This effectively writes "enhancing environmental construction" into the 13th five-year plan (2016—2020), the blueprint for China's immediate economic and social priorities. This embedding of environmental concerns into the plan is thought to be the first time in history, since the first five-year plan in 1953. For more details, please see the website http://finance.qq.com/a/20151025/026983.htm.

of thoughts are cultural roots and spiritual homes from which China should never depart. On 26 January, 2017, the *People's Daily* published a long article revolving around the guidelines for fully preserving, rejuvenating, developing and promoting traditional Chinese culture, jointly issued by the General Office of the Communist Party of China Central Committee, and the General Office of the State Council. The guidelines call for traditional culture-oriented research, inheritance, protection, innovation, education and exchange so as to fulfil a "marked boost" in the international diffusion and influence of Chinese culture by 2025.① Therefore, my ecopoetical translations of the Confucian text *Dizigui* and the Daoist canon *Daodejing* charged with ecological visions can be regarded as a significant response both to escalating ecological challenges, and to the call for cultural confidence, rejuvenation and dissemination that underlie the "Belt and Road Initiative".

① For more details, please see "Guidelines for Implementing the Project of Inheriting and Developing Excellent Traditional Chinese Culture"：关于实施中华优秀传统文化传承发展工程的意见 [N/OL]. People's Daily (2017-01-26) [2017-08-03]. http://paper.people.com.cn/rmrb/html/2017-01/26/nw.D110000renmrb_20170126_1-06.htm.

Within this intracultural and transcultural framework of anthropocenic ecopoetics, I argue that *Dizigui* (*Standards for Disciples*, the main concern of this book) as an important literary text embodies a great number of phenomenological, political, social, cultural, educational and ecological values that speak themselves to the harsh environmental realities that confront us in the Anthropocene. Its meanings and values are open to exploration and discussion. Different readers with varied background knowledge and expertise can approach and interpret this book in their own manner. At this junction, it is necessary to briefly introduce *Dizigui*. As the title suggests, it is a primer about the standards and guidelines of behaviour for students, widely known as a compendium of traditional Chinese family instructions, disciplines and education. It was named *Xunmengwen* (*Admonishments for Disciples*) written by Yuxiu Li (李毓秀, 1647—1729), a Xiucai (one who passed the imperial examination at the local level) during the reign of Emperor Kangxi in the Qing Dynasty. Later on, Li's contemporary scholar Cunren Jia (贾存仁) revised Li's work and renamed it as the current title. Li, however, is widely considered as the author of this text about conduct. As a scholar and educator in the early Qing Dynasty, he intensively studied the Confucian classics *The Great Learning* and *Doctrine of the Mean*, and set up a lecture hall. What he taught in the hall was basically Confucian ideas. Sensitive to the serious illiteracy problems with adult farmers, Li decided to compose a primer that enabled them to learn. He based the essential ideas of the primer *Dizigui* on the sixth chapter from the first part of the widely-known Confucian canon *The Analects*, and then developed and expanded those ideas to seven chapters together with a preamble.

Li's primer is functional both for its literary values, and for its primary educational goal of imparting knowledge to farmers so as to refine their behaviour and humanity. It has 1080 words in total, comprising 360 lines. There are three characters in each line, resembling the artistic techniques of another Chinese classic entitled *Sanzijing* (*The Three-Character Primer*). Its special cadence characterized by beautiful musical rhythms and varied rhyming patterns facilitates memorization and recitation. Although the original objects of Li's teaching were illiterate adult farmers, the term “disciple” (as the title of the book suggests) during and before the Qing Dynasty merely meant young students in **Sishu** (private schools). This contradiction indicates that *Dizigui* aims at elucidating the standards of conduct to students of all ages in the hope that they could behave well indoors and outdoors. In this regard, we can expand the definition of “disciple” in our age to cover children at home, students at schools and universities, employees in companies, and adults in rural and urban communities at large. In other words, it can refer to all inhabitants of the Earth. Therefore, *Dizigui* serves as a significant guide book for individuals of our age to better and purify their selves, and cultivate and enhance their ecological sensibilities that underpin family, social, and environmental duties. The implications of applying this book in this way are so broad that I can only attempt in what follows to explore certain inflections of *Dizigui* values in light of the current epoch.

Human behaviours are innately related to and largely influenced by their worldviews. To shape and enhance humanity’s ecological sensibilities requires the implanting of the seeds of morality and virtues into their minds.

Learning this enlightening Chinese educational primer will help modern readers to reshape their minds with moral teachings, and to double-check or ameliorate their conducts so as to avoid moral degradation and demerits. Just as a quatrain from the first Chapter titled "Filial Duties Indoors" admonishes:

Although things small,
do not act.
If you act,
your virtues fall.

The lines above emphasize the importance of being a virtuous inhabitant. Li's original objective through this teaching is to encourage children never to do anything wicked and trivial as we wrongly consider, otherwise they will be morally degraded and unfilial, and their parents will feel unhappy and even ashamed. In view of current ecological crises, this Confucian moral admonishment can actually imply that individuals, as offsprings of Mother Earth, should never do anything harmful to ecospheres, including some actions of which we are usually unconscious, regarding them as trivialities like water and food waste, firewood harvesting and burning, littering, to name but a few.

If the previous stanza displays a Confucian discouragement from small devil acts, then one of the main motifs that underlie the whole book actually encourages us to believe that goodness and benevolence come from accumulative small acts of morality. Although acts are separately small-scale and even minuscule, they, once accumulated, will generate big changes. There is an echo of the view expressed by Her Majesty Queen Elizabeth Ⅱ when delivering her 2016 Christmas Message: "it's understandable that we sometimes think the world's problems are so big that we can do little to help. On our own, we cannot end wars or wipe out injustice, but the cumulative impact of thousands of small acts of goodness can be bigger than we imagine"[①]. Concerning environmental problems in the Anthropocene, albeit too huge and complex to address completely in one go, which renders us now and then

① The Guardian. The Queen's 2016 Christmas Message[EB/OL]. [2016-12-25]. https://www.theguardian.com/uk-news/2016/dec/25/the-queens-speech-christmas-day-full-transcript-elizabeth.

helpless, we should retain an unceasing hope and belief that the world will become better and more beneficial insofar as humanity transform themselves steadily for better by virtue of accumulative minor conducts of constructive benevolence.

As a formative educational guide, *Dizigui* through a broad-based cultural transfer offers pupils and students manifold ideas that are expected to broaden their world outlook and life values. For example, in the second chapter named "Good Brother Outdoors", the opening lines register the importance of harmonious brotherhood and a spirit of cooperation:

Older care younger,
younger respect older.
Live in peace,
feuds will cease.

These lines also imply that a sense of thankfulness and love should mushroom among brothers and sisters so that disputes will be avoided, and happiness and peace will be achieved, bolstered, and magnified. This is reminiscent of what Her Majesty, Queen Elizabeth II reminded us in her

2015 Christmas speech: "it inspires us to try harder: to be thankful for the people who bring love and happiness into our own lives, and to look for ways of spreading that love to others, whenever and wherever we can"[①]. Thus, to build harmonious social communities and environments, which is an essential marker and ultimate goal of social ecology, love and respect are urgently needed in our age and should not only be educated among children but also encouraged and reinforced among people across borders and cultures, especially in the age of rampant commercialism aligned with neo-isolationism as a result of Brexit and America-first policies.

Additionally, *Dizigui* is still valuable in that it suggests that students at various ages should keep their own indoor environments orderly and clean:

Keep rooms clean,
walls tidy scene.
Keep desks uncluttered,
brushes 'n inkstones ordered.

---

① The Guardian. The Queen's 2015 Christmas Message[EB/OL]. [2016-12-25]. http://www.bbc.co.uk/news/uk-35178485.

They are encouraged to maintain a clean environment and keep their daily indoor life in order so that their minds will not be distracted by messiness. Brushes and inkstones in this case are for sure traditionally Chinese culture-loaded terms. Students from other countries, however, when reading these unfamiliar items, can still understand what this stanza means and advocates by naturally associating them with their own familiar stationery like a pen and a pencil box. Considering the cultivation of environmental sensibilities in humanity, we may find that the quoted lines also suggest that humans who are able to keep their indoor homes tidy and clean are largely inclined to virtuously manage the outdoor homes well, particularly the one of Mother Nature.

Dizigui also teaches students how to learn effectively and consistently: "What learning requires?/ Three things heeded:/ Heart, eyes, mouth./ Faith also needed." In ancient and contemporary Chinese education, teachers usually stress students' deployment of multiple senses from different organs, such as eyes, ears, nose, mouth, and mind to achieve productive learning. Students are required never to be absent-minded but to pay full attention in class. However, what is somewhat disappointing concerning the current status quo in British education is that students more often than not fail to demonstrate full attention in class. The difference between Chinese and British students in classroom behaviour has been well filmed and explored by the BBC series of educational programmes named "Are Our Kids Tough Enough? Chinese School" broadcast in BBC Two in late summer, 2015. As the programmes show, five Chinese teachers were hired to teach 50 British pupils at Bohunt School in Hampshire by adopting traditional Chinese pedagogical approaches. The local students in the first place felt uncomfortable with this full-attention-required method and could not get accustomed to this intensive learning. They frolicked around and chatted with desk mates, displaying behaviour which would seldom be seen in a class in China. Classroom discipline is needed, just as Ms Yang, one of the five teachers, stressed in class to students, "Discipline is really important. Without discipline, you can't learn well". In China, normally there is no need for teachers to repeat classroom disciplines since students are cognitive of how to behave well in class. The situation, however, is quite different in the UK. As we can see in the programme, five teachers in the first place strenuously struggled to control the classroom. They repeated strict classroom disciplines all the time that require students' "heart, eyes, mouth" full attention. As time rolled by, the students gradually got used to this disciplined learning environment. Mutual understanding between teachers and students grew, and the classroom harmony was gradually established. To the surprise of Mr Strowger, Bohunt Headmaster, and the students' parents, the result of the examinations given by the third evaluation institute and seated by the students with Chinese teaching styles and those with British ones became disparate, with the former achieving better scores than the latter. The case provided here is not to suggest that the Chinese educational system is better than the British, but it does make us reflect on the significance and necessity of full attention in class. In light of environmental protection, these lines also inform that humans, when learning and unravelling the nature and root causes of ecological crises, need full attention in order to find desirable, effective and comprehensive solutions.

There are some guidelines in *Dizigui* that will for sure arouse the resistance of contemporary students, especially Western ones. For example, in the first chapter, there is a stanza that urges students to fulfil their filial duties to parents:

Whatever parents like,
fulfil their dream.
Whatever they dislike,
avoid any scheme.

With no background knowledge of the importance that we Chinese attach to the tradition of **Xiao** (traditionally translated as filial piety, but I equate it with filial duties throughout this book), students will ask similar questions like Sophie in the aforementioned BBC programme who questioned Ms Yang. When the latter insisted in class, "Your parents are always right", the former challenged by asking what if parents asked them to do something bad and immoral. Ms Yang's words which reflect that she's strongly influenced by and strictly adhered to that tradition are the echo of what the *Dizigui* guidelines believe, "Whatever parents like, / fulfil their dream". Normally Chinese students presuppose that their parents would not ask them to do anything immoral since Chinese **Xiao** tradition always encourages children not to do anything against law and morality, which is also evident throughout *Dizigui*. British students, however, influenced by individualism that values rights and freedom, and tends to encourage challenging authority, may naturally resist this Chinese precept.

Although the guidelines we have analysed above may sound more educational-oriented than ecological-based, there are some lines in *Dizigui* which do directly and strongly encourage the cultivation of humanity's environmental sensibilities:

Man in feeling
love every being.
Same Heaven share;
same Earth bear.

This stanza advocates environmental justice, equal rights and philanthropy for every being in global ecospheres. This is conducive to the ecological enterprise in our age of Anthropocenic ecological spiritual crisis by challenging dominant and prevailing Cartesian dualism, hierarchical hubris and strong anthropocentrism that justify Homo sapiens' exploitation of non-human beings.

It is noteworthy that there is no image of the sun in the original stanza, only that of man, heaven and earth. Thus, my rendering, if adding "the sun", would mislead readers to the interpretation that the original piece implies the possibility of and allowance for unseemly activities taking place in the moon-lit night. This tends to decrease readers' environmental sensibility of environmental justice to all beings at all times, a belief that the original text intends to emphasize. Besides, if my translation simply employed "nature" and "creature" to replace "heaven" and "earth" in my eagerness to find a pair of rhymes, it would not only be somewhat unfaithful to the source-language images but also arouse heated discussion about the identiy issue around the Creator (God, Allah, or Chinese Pan Gu and Nǚ Wa), which is not the intention of the original stanza. Because the original piece simply highlights the environmental interdependence between humans and non-human entities. In this ecological sense, my closely-rhymed and concise version sounds faithful to the original quatrain in ideorealm and aesthetics.

Man-made and urban environment is a major ecological concern nowadays in the age of increasing urbanization. Since urban planning policies indirectly or directly affect our urban habits and lifestyle, architects, urban planners and policymakers should shoulder more responsibilities and initiatives to secure inhabitable and environmentally friendly urban areas. They need take cultural elements into consideration when conducting urban planning. As Christopher highlights in his monograph *Urban Ecology*, "ecologically based urban planning can widely benefit from cultural analyses" ①. *Dizigui* is surely an important source of cultural analysis that can teach planners and policymakers

① SCHLIEPHAKE C. Urban Ecologies: City Space, Material Agency, and Environmental Politics in Contemporary Culture [M]. London: Lexington Books, 2014: 192.

to restrain their destructive ideas. In China, *Dizigui* has in recent years seen its own increasing popularity with students, parents, and white-collar workers in cities, who hope to be instructed by its Confucian teachings to become good ecological citizens. In this sense, I firmly believe that this primer can offer some urban ecological wisdom in light of Western urban ecologies. Therefore, Christopher, as an expert in this field, is definitely in a good position to write such a prism in his preface.

The special nature of this translation work calls for some explanations. The source-language text and target-language renderings assembled here are the result of roughly four years' reading, searching, meditation, and translation. In this book, two types of renderings are offered, viz., a poetic version and an interpretative one. The interpretative version is based on my draft translation initiated in 2012. At the early stage, I had to understand and decode the very condensed and concise literary Chinese first before translating them into English. Consequently, a couple of hours was spent on this task every day, and it took me over one year to finish it. Later on, I was forced to set the interpretative translations aside because I had to pursue my PhD degree in the UK. Due to the heavy doctoral workloads, I unfortunately did not have time to revamp that first draft of interpretative translation. However, in the light of the current heated discussion, home and abroad, of the relativity of Chinese classics to our current age and the coming fourth wave of translation in Chinese academia characterized by a large number of Chinese scholars and translators with increasingly ardent passions for Chinese classic texts in response to the call of "B&R Initiative", I began to envisage how I could contribute to this wave. Correspondingly, I started the poetic version on April 15th, 2016. Also triggered by the concerns about the linguistic clumsiness and archaism, and the unfaithfulness in meaning that characterize some of the previously existing renderings of *Dizigui*, I decided to transform my interpretative renderings into a poetic form. With the help of my previous prose translations, it is easier and less time-consuming to accomplish the poetic version. However, it is still quite energy-and-effort-consuming to maintain the formal equivalence. Since the source-language stanza has four lines (a poetic form), I maintain the poetic quatrain in the rendering as well. As the original line has three characters, three words are harnessed in the target-language text. Besides, the rhyming scheme of almost all Chinese stanzas is basically ABCB and there are some exceptions such as the first stanza in the preamble with a rhyme pattern being ABCD, and some other stanzas being ABAB, ABBB, AABA, and AABB. Therefore, most of my poetic renderings are rhymed, predominantly adopting the patterns like ABCB and ABAB, with occational exceptions ABBA, AABB, AABA and AAAA. Apart from the concerns of formal fidelity, the rhymed and concise renderings, as I hope, can allow students of all ages (at least young children) to easily remember and recite them so that they can accept this Chinese canon wholeheartedly. Sometimes it is very likely for a translator to overvalue some elements like metrical rhythms and rhymes at the cost of others like substance and meaning. Thus, to avoid a dualism between substance and form, I endeavour in my renderings to balance them in a well-structured organic way. To this end, under each poetic rendering, the interpretative version is kept as a kind of note and explanation in the hope that it can clarify the points that the original and poetic versions sometimes might fail to convey and may be obscure to twenty-first-century readers, and can better their understandings. Suffice to note that both poetic and interpretative renderings serve to reproduce the original texts as living and organic works. In this sense, I hope that my translations can be envisioned as an arena of literary and cultural rejuvenation, travelling through the target-language context and our current era, of this Chinese text written more than three centuries ago. Chinese Pinyin Romanization (pronunciation of Chinese characters) is also provided under each rendering so that it enables a handy study of Chinese Mandarin.

Ultimately, it is in principle conceivable and hopeful that this multimodal book could help enhance the cultural exchange between Chinese and other communities. It is my fervent hope that scholars and students of Eastern-

Western humanities, especially China studies, eco-literature, translation studies, and pedagogy will find this book an engaging and meaningful reference.

Initially written at Menai View Terrace, Bangor

23/04/2016 — 03/12/2017

Revised by White Clouds Mountain, Guangzhou

01/10/2019 — 15/11/2019

目　录

CONTENTS

zǒng xù
总叙

Proem

The *Dizigui*: All Chapters

Written by Ray Murphy

The Philosopher's words fall to the ground
Descending just as trees shed autumn leaves
To nourish the earthly fundament new
From dying embers rise honest virtue

《弟子规》：总叙

瑞蒙·莫菲 作

许景城 译

先哲语，坠地声，

萧萧树，落叶秋，

润瘠土，春又生，

灰烬处，德不休。

dì zǐ guī
弟子规

shèng rén xùn
圣人训

shǒu xiào tì
首孝悌

cì jǐn xìn
次谨信

【 Poetic English Version 】

The disciples' preachings,
our sages' teachings!
First, be dutiful. (Duties come first.)
Second, be careful. (Credits go dispersed.)

【 Interpretative English Version 】 The guidelines for disciples are the teachings inherited from such ancient Chinese sages as Confucius. Firstly, shoulder filial duties and show respects to your parents and elder siblings. Secondly, be cautious and trustworthy in your daily life.

fàn ài zhòng
泛爱众

ér qīn rén
而亲仁

yǒu yú lì
有余力

zé xué wén
则学文

【Poetic English Version】

Third, love all. (Love beings all.)
Virtues, don't stall.
Lastly, learn arts (Go learn arts)
as gift starts.

【Interpretative English Version】 Thirdly, be devoted to loving all beings equally, adhering to great virtues and goodness. Finally, be dedicated to literature and arts as your gift starts working and time allows.

dì yī zhāng　　rù zé xiào

第一章　入则孝

Chapter 1　Filial Duties Indoors

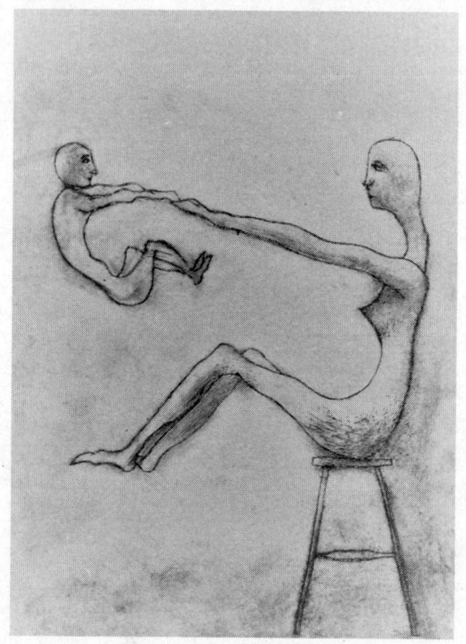

On Filial Duty

Written by Ray Murphy

When we were young and all the world seemed safe
The parents gazed on gilded carefree child
As one grows aged in a harmful globe
Will duty return to protect their fading

论　孝

瑞蒙·莫菲　作

许景城　译

垂髫时，世安泰，

父母视，金童淘。

世间险，人渐衰，

道义返，侍奉老？

fù mǔ hū
父母呼

yìng wù huǎn
应勿缓

fù mǔ mìng
父母命

xíng wù lǎn
行勿懒

【Poetic English Version】

When parents adjure,
please respond promptly.
When they require,
please act quickly.

【Interpretative English Version】 Respond promptly to parents' calls and requirements. Never be indolent.

fù mǔ jiào
父母教

xū jìng tīng
须敬听

fù mǔ zé
父母责

xū shùn chéng
须顺承

【 **Poetic English Version** 】

When parents declaim,
lend your ears.
When they blame,
accept strict steers.

【 **Interpretative English Version** 】Give respectful ears to your parents' instructions. Take a compliant approach to your parents' reproach.

dōng zé wēn
冬则温

xià zé qìng
夏则凊

chén zé xǐng
晨则省

hūn zé dìng
昏则定

【 Poetic English Version 】

Warm in winter;
cool in summer.
At morn, greet;
good night, bid.

【 Interpretative English Version 】 Warm your parents in winter, and cool them in summer. Greet them cheerily in the morning, and wish them sincerely "Good Night".

chū bì gào
出必告

fǎn bì miàn
反必面

jū yǒu cháng
居有常

yè wú biàn
业无变

【 Poetic English Version 】

Going and coming,
report trip range.
A constant dwelling.
Jobs never change.

【 Interpretative English Version 】 Allay parents' concerns by telling them your agenda when you plan to go out, and by reporting to them after you return. Maintain your lifestyle, dwelling, and occupation constant. Never change them willfully.

shì suī xiǎo
事虽小

wù shàn wéi
勿擅为

gǒu shàn wéi
苟擅为

zǐ dào kuī
子道亏

【Poetic English Version】

Although things small,
do not act.
If you act,
your virtues fall.

【Interpretative English Version】 Never do anything that seems trivial. If you do, you will be morally degraded and unfilial, as your parents will feel unhappy and ashamed.

wù suī xiǎo
物虽小

wù sī cáng
勿私藏

gǒu sī cáng
苟私藏

qīn xīn shāng
亲心伤

【Poetic English Version】

Although things small,
do not stash.
If you stash,
parents' hearts fall.

【Interpretative English Version】 Never illegally stash anything even if it seems small, for if you do, your parents will be heartbroken.

qīn suǒ hào
亲所好

lì wèi jù
力为具

qīn suǒ wù
亲所恶

jǐn wèi qù
谨为去

【Poetic English Version】

Whatever parents like,
fulfill their dream.
Whatever they dislike,
avoid any scheme.

【Interpretative English Version】 Try your best reasonably to do whatever your parents like. Try your best carefully to avoid doing whatever your parents dislike.

shēn yǒu shāng
身有伤

yí qīn yōu
贻亲忧

dé yǒu shāng
德有伤

yí qīn xiū
贻亲羞

【 Poetic English Version 】

Injured your body,
parents feel pain.
Your virtues bawdy,
they bear shame.

【 Interpretative English Version 】 Never worry your parents by sloppily injuring your body. Never shame your parents by carelessly ruining your virtues.

qīn ài wǒ
亲爱我

xiào hé nán
孝何难

qīn wù wǒ
亲恶我 *

xiào fāng xián
孝方贤

* 另有版本为“亲憎我”。

【 Poetic English Version 】

Parents love you!
Love them filially.
They grudge you?
Love them stably.

【 Interpretative English Version 】 Never be reluctant to show filial duties to your parents who love you. Never be improper to test your filial duties to your parents who bear a grudge against you.

qīn yǒu guò
亲有过

jiàn shǐ gēng
谏使更

yí wú sè
怡吾色

róu wú shēng
柔吾声

【Poetic English Version】

If they erred,
give good choices,
but with smile,
in soft voices.

【Interpretative English Version】 Exhort your parents to change for better if they have faults, but do so with a smiling face and in an amiable voice.

jiàn bù rù
谏不入

yuè fù jiàn
悦复谏

hào qì suí
号泣随

tà wú yuàn
挞无怨

【 Poetic English Version 】

They don’t listen?
Remonstrate when pleasant.
Tears move them.
Always no resentment.

【 Interpretative English Version 】 If parents do not accept your advice, please wait until their mood is cheery and remonstrate again. Please use tears to exhort them if necessary. Never abhor them if they whip you.

qīn yǒu jí
亲有疾

yào xiān cháng
药先尝

zhòu yè shì
昼夜侍

bù lí chuáng
不离床

【 Poetic English Version 】

When they're ill,
try their pill.
Day 'n night care,
by sickbed fare.

【 Interpretative English Version 】 Taste the medication first before giving it to your ailing parents. Attend them by their bedside day and night.

sāng sān nián
丧三年

cháng bēi yè
常悲咽

jū chù biàn
居处变

jiǔ ròu jué
酒肉绝

【 **Poetic English Version** 】

Mourn three years,
by parents' shrine.
Change living spheres,
avoid meat 'n wine.

【 **Interpretative English Version** 】 Mourn them always in sorrow and gratitude for three years after their death. Avoid festivities even if your abode is changed.

sāng jìn lǐ
丧尽礼

jì jìn chéng
祭尽诚

shì sǐ zhě
事死者

rú shì shēng
如事生

【Poetic English Version】

Hold funerals rightly.
Worship them sincerely.
Respect still politely,
as before dearly.

【Interpretative English Version】 Arrange parents' funerals with the greatest etiquette, and commemorate them with the greatest sincerity. Then revere them as if they were still alive.

dì èr zhāng chū zé tì
第二章 出则悌

Chapter 2 Good Brothers Outdoors

Parenthood

Written by Ray Murphy

The restless waves, wash away our dreams,
Played out in footsteps across billowing strand.
Our duty done, offspring leave, sans backward glance,
As we wait on the ebbtide of vanished life.

为人父母

瑞蒙·莫菲 作

许景城 译

海汹涌，梦冲淹，
滚浑洪，袭拍岸。
子女长，弃不顾，
落潮边，独寡孤。

xiōng dào yǒu
兄道友

dì dào gōng
弟道恭

xiōng dì mù
兄弟睦

xiào zài zhōng
孝在中

【Poetic English Version】

Older care younger,
younger respect older.
Live in peace,
feuds will cease.

【Interpretative English Version】Older children should care about younger ones. Younger siblings should respect older ones. Be harmonious with one another and consequently filial to parents.

cái wù qīng
财物轻

yuàn hé shēng
怨何生

yán yǔ rěn
言语忍

fèn zì mǐn
忿自泯

【Poetic English Version】

Value wealth less,
gain joy more.
More calmly express,
less troubles draw.

【Interpretative English Version】 Value family bonds more importantly than wealth so that no hatred will arise. Be patient to the person you are conversing with so as to cause no trouble or anger.

huò yǐn shí
或饮食

huò zuò zǒu
或坐走

zhǎng zhě xiān
长者先

yòu zhě hòu
幼者后

【 Poetic English Version 】

Eating or drinking,
sitting or walking,
elders go leading;
youngers are following.

【 Interpretative English Version 】 Let the elder go first and the younger follow when drinking, eating, sitting or walking.

zhǎng hū rén
长呼人

jí dài jiào
即代叫

rén bú zài
人不在

jǐ jí dào
己即到

【 Poetic English Version 】

Elders call someone?
Go and seek.
They're not found?
Return and speak.

【 Interpretative English Version 】 If elders call and need someone, you should go and seek. If he or she cannot be found, you should return and report your results.

chēng zūn zhǎng
称尊长

wù hū míng
勿呼名

duì zūn zhǎng
对尊长

wù xiàn néng
勿见能

【 Poetic English Version 】

Call the elders,
not in disgrace.
Don't be braggers,
to their face.

【 Interpretative English Version 】 Never address elders by their given names. Never show off in their presence.

lù yù zhǎng
路遇长

jí qū yī
疾趋揖

zhǎng wú yán
长无言

tuì gōng lì
退恭立

【Poetic English Version】

Elders upon meeting,

please bow promptly.

They aren't reacting?

Please stand straightly.

【Interpretative English Version】 Bow to elders respectfully and promptly when encountering them. Stand back or aside venerably even if they do not greet back.

qí xià mǎ
骑下马

chéng xià chē
乘下车

guò yóu dài
过犹待

bǎi bù yú
百步余

【Poetic English Version】

Seeing them ahead,
alight from cars;
wait, let pass
until not beheld.

【Interpretative English Version】 Alight from your carriage and give elders a ride if spotting them walking on route. Stop your carriage and wait until they pass by and disappear from sight.

zhǎng zhě lì
长者立

yòu wù zuò
幼勿坐

zhǎng zhě zuò
长者坐

mìng nǎi zuò
命乃坐

【Poetic English Version】

If they stand,
do not sit.
If they're seated,
sit on command.

【Interpretative English Version】 Never be seated when an elder is standing. Sit down at the request of those who are sitting.

zūn zhǎng qián
尊长前

shēng yào dī
声要低

dī bù wén
低不闻

què fēi yí
却非宜

【Poetic English Version】

Elders stand by?
Lower your voice.
Hearing no reply,
retreat? Bad choice!

【Interpretative English Version】 Speak slowly and softly when conversing with elders. It is inappropriate to feel embarrassed and retreat if you do not make yourself heard.

jìn bì qū
进必趋

tuì bì chí
退必迟

wèn qǐ duì
问起对

shì wù yí
视勿移

【Poetic English Version】

Arriving or retreating,
always follow by.
Asked and answering,
eye to eye.

【Interpretative English Version】 Receive an elder promptly when arriving, and retreat slowly when leaving. Look into his or her eyes when answering questions raised by an elder.

shì zhū fù
事诸父

rú shì fù
如事父

shì zhū xiōng
事诸兄

rú shì xiōng
如事兄

【Poetic English Version】

Treat others' fathers,

like your own.

Treat others' brothers,

as at home.

【Interpretative English Version】 Serve everyone's parents the same as you do to your own. Treat others' brothers the same as your own.

dì sān zhāng jǐn
第三章 谨

Chapter 3 Carefulness

Perilous Water

Written by Ray Murphy

Deep runs the water that is the sea
Flows benign, yet makes ready swift to rage
Pounding with rising, windswept tide, to leave
Virtue afloat, yet sailor with a sinking heart

激 流

瑞蒙·莫菲 作

许景城 译

水深澈，犹海中，
波清洌，亦激涌，
浪砰磅，风潮卷，
德浮荡，船夫惘。

zhāo qǐ zǎo
朝起早

yè mián chí
夜眠迟

lǎo yì zhì
老易至

xī cǐ shí
惜此时

【Poetic English Version】

Rise at morn,
sleep late night.
Ageing, fast song,
cherish time right.

【Interpretative English Version】 Get up at dawn and go to bed late. Cherish time right and keenly since life is transient and aging is fast.

chén bì guàn
晨必盥

jiān shù kǒu
兼漱口

biàn nì huí
便溺回

zhé jìng shǒu
辄净手

【Poetic English Version】

Wash at morn,
gargle as well.
After natural horn,
wash hands well.

【Interpretative English Version】 In the morning, wash your face and brush your teeth after getting up. Wash your hands soon after the natural call.

guān bì zhèng
冠必正

niǔ bì jié
纽必结

wà yǔ lǚ
袜与履

jù jǐn qiè
俱紧切

【 Poetic English Version 】

Straighten your hat.
Fasten buttons right.
Wear socks pat.
Tie shoes tight.

【 Interpretative English Version 】 Straighten your hat, fasten your buttons and snaps, and tie up your socks and shoes neatly.

zhì guān fú
置冠服

yǒu dìng wèi
有定位

wù luàn dùn
勿乱顿

zhì wū huì
致污秽

【Poetic English Version】

Hats and dress,
in right place;
not in mess,
nor in disgrace.

【Interpretative English Version】 Wear or put away your hat and garments in the right places. Never leave them disordered and stained.

yī guì jié
衣贵洁

bù guì huá
不贵华

shàng xún fèn
上循分

xià chèn jiā
下称家

【 Poetic English Version 】

What're good clothes?
Cleanness not fashion.
Outdoors proper shows,
indoors family notion.

【 Interpretative English Version 】 Neat and clean clothes are more important than luxurious and fashionable ones. In public, wear proper garments in accordance with your status and occassion, leaving a good impression. At home, wear garbs in accordance with your family custom.

duì yǐn shí
对饮食

wù jiǎn zé
勿拣择

shí shì kě
食适可

wù guò zé
勿过则

【Poetic English Version】

Food and drink,

do not complain!

Eat and think:

I should abstain!

【Interpretative English Version】 Never pick or grumble about food and drink given to you. Never over-eat. Please abstain.

nián fāng shào
年方少

wù yǐn jiǔ
勿饮酒

yǐn jiǔ zuì
饮酒醉

zuì wéi chǒu
最为丑

【Poetic English Version】

Young in age,
never touch wine.
Drinking till rage,
vice will shine.

【Interpretative English Version】 Never drink alcohol when you are young. Alcohol abuse will bring you a great disgrace.

bù cóng róng
步从容

lì duān zhèng
立端正

yī shēn yuán
揖深圆

bài gōng jìng
拜恭敬

【 Poetic English Version 】

Walk in poise,
stand well upright.
Bow with joys,
kowtow just right.

【 Interpretative English Version 】 Pace your steps politely when walking, and straighten up your back gracefully when standing. Perfect your bow with respect and joy, and kneel down to show your courtesy.

wù jiàn yù
勿践阈

wù bǒ yǐ
勿跛倚

wù jī jù
勿箕踞

wù yáo bì
勿摇髀

【Poetic English Version】

Do not swagger.
Do not stagger.
Sit, don't splay!
Hip, don't sway!

【Interpretative English Version】 Never tread or tramp, nor stagger or crawl. Never sprawl out when sitting, or sway your hip when walking.

huǎn jiē lián
缓揭帘

wù yǒu shēng
勿有声

kuān zhuǎn wān
宽转弯

wù chù léng
勿触棱

【Poetic English Version】

Pull curtains slowly;
make no noise.
Turn at ease;
avoid corners wholly.

【Interpretative English Version】 Roll curtains up carefully and quietly. Turn at the corner of a room and never run into it.

zhí xū qì
执虚器

rú zhí yíng
如执盈

rù xū shì
入虚室

rú yǒu rén
如有人

[Poetic English Version]

Hold empty glass,
like in boom.
Enter empty room,
like owners pass.

[Interpretative English Version] Hold an empty pot carefully as if it were full. Enter an empty room meticulously as if it were occupied or its owner passed around. Thus, we should be careful.

shì wù máng
事勿忙

máng duō cuò
忙多错

wù wèi nán
勿畏难

wù qīng lüè
勿轻略

【 Poetic English Version 】

To avoid flaws,
don't hasten course!
Fear no trouble;
ignore no nibble.

【 Interpretative English Version 】 Never hasten your affairs or course; otherwise it is easy to make mistakes. Never fear the difficulty; nor neglect the easy.

dòu nào chǎng
斗闹场

jué wù jìn
绝勿近

xié pì shì
邪僻事

jué wù wèn
绝勿问

【 Poetic English Version 】

Any rowdy place,
keep distant space.
Any evil fire,
do not acquire.

【 Interpretative English Version 】 Keep away from rowdy quarters, such as casinos, bars and brothels. Never enquire about anything unusual and evil.

jiāng rù mén
将入门

wèn shú cún
问孰存

jiāng shàng táng
将上堂

shēng bì yáng
声必扬

【 Poetic English Version 】

Knock or call,
before you enter.
Make sound better,
in meeting hall.

【 Interpretative English Version 】 Knock at the door or call for permission before entering a house. Make yourself heard with measured sound in a conference hall.

rén wèn shuí
人问谁

duì yǐ míng
对以名

wú yǔ wǒ
吾与我

bù fēn míng
不分明

【Poetic English Version】

Asked to view,

first your name.

"Me" or "You",

not clear aim.

【Interpretative English Version】 Respond by telling your name when asked. Be careful not just to respond by saying "Me" or "Oh, it's me", for it is not good enough to get yourself known.

yòng rén wù
用人物

xū míng qiú
须明求

tǎng bú wèn
倘不问

jí wéi tōu
即为偷

【Poetic English Version】

To use something,
ask for allowance.
With no asking,
you're in defiance.

【Interpretative English Version】 Ask for permission before using others' possessions. You make yourself a thief if you do not ask for allowance.

jiè rén wù
借人物

jí shí huán
及时还

rén jiè wù
人借物

yǒu wù qiān
有勿悭*

---

* 另有版本“后有急　借不难”。

【Poetic English Version】

Return in time
what you prime.
If someone borrows,
no meanness shows.

【Interpretative English Version】 Return them in time after priming others' possessions you borrow; if someone comes to borrow your belongings, please don't be mean but be generous.

dì sì zhāng xìn
第四章　信

Chapter 4 Honesty

Vanishing Resource

Written by Ray Murphy

The Miner digs and treads through fossilized seams
Dredging the resource of a consuming State
Coal is King, while its subject breathless toils
The honest man in a careless world

资源枯竭

瑞蒙·莫菲　作

许景城　译

化石缝，劳役凿，

宝矿逢，掘取捞。

煤至上，难呼吸，

世间寒，诚者凄。

fán chū yán
凡出言

xìn wéi xiān
信为先

zhà yǔ wàng
诈与妄

xī kě yān
奚可焉

【Poetic English Version】

When you talk,
do not lie.
Craft and stalk,
do not apply.

【Interpretative English Version】 Be honest with what you say in communication with others. Never cheat or brag.

huà shuō duō
话说多

bù rú shǎo
不如少

wéi qí shì
惟其是

wù nìng qiǎo
勿佞巧

【Poetic English Version】

Don't talk much,
when asked such.
Only speak truth.
Do not smutch!

【Interpretative English Version】 In some occasions, speaking little is better than talking too much. Only speak truth and never embroider facts.

kè bó yǔ
刻薄语*

huì wū cí
秽污词

shì jǐng qì
市井气

qiè jiè zhī
切戒之

* 另有版本为“奸巧语”。

【 Poetic English Version 】

No cunning pity.
No dirty words.
No gaudy vanity.
Avoid bad records.

【 Interpretative English Version 】 Never say four-letter, dirty or obscene words. Avoid unseemly behaviours in any case.

jiàn wèi zhēn
见未真

wù qīng yán
勿轻言

zhī wèi dì
知未的

wù qīng chuán
勿轻传

【 Poetic English Version 】

Do not misread
without seeing truth.
Do not spread
words of untruth.

【 Interpretative English Version 】 Never tell others what you do not see with your own eyes. Never spread what you are unsure of.

shì fēi yí
事非宜

wù qīng nuò
勿轻诺

gǒu qīng nuò
苟轻诺

jìn tuì cuò
进退错

【Poetic English Version】

Do not promise
what is wrong.
If you promise,
troubles come along.

【Interpretative English Version】 Never promise to fulfil any tasks that are actually wrong and unreasonable. If you promise, you will put yourself in a quandary.

fán dào zì
凡道字

zhòng qiě shū
重且舒

wù jí jí
勿急疾

wù mó hu
勿模糊

【Poetic English Version】

Highlight main points,
when you speak.
No hasty critique.
No vague viewpoints.

【Interpretative English Version】 Speak words emphatically and smoothly, not hastily or ambiguously.

bǐ shuō cháng
彼说长

cǐ shuō duǎn
此说短

bù guān jǐ
不关己

mò xián guǎn
莫闲管

【Poetic English Version】

Some like praising.

Some like carping.

Not our business!

Stay away please!

【Interpretative English Version】 Some would like to speak well of others while some are inclined to speak ill of others. Never involve yourself in any talk that should have nothing to do with you.

jiàn rén shàn
见人善

jí sī qí
即思齐

zòng qù yuǎn
纵去远

yǐ jiàn jī
以渐跻

【Poetic English Version】

Follow the mind
of good speech.
Though far behind,
strive to reach.

【Interpretative English Version】 Follow those whose merits shine brightly. Though you are left far behind, please be confident and strive to catch up.

jiàn rén è
见人恶

jí nèi xǐng
即内省

yǒu zé gǎi
有则改

wú jiā jǐng
无加警

【Poetic English Version】

When seeing demerits,
brooding won't hurt.
Correct bad credits.
Always keep alert.

【Interpretative English Version】 Examine yourself when you see others' faults. If you have similar demerits, correct them. If not, try to be alert.

wéi dé xué
唯德学

wéi cái yì
唯才艺

bù rú rén
不如人

dāng zì lì
当自砺

【 Poetic English Version 】

Virtue and nature,
talent and skill.
If lower still,
try to nurture!

【 Interpretative English Version 】 Work harder to improve your virtue, knowledge, talent and skill, if you find them inferior.

ruò yī fú
若衣服

ruò yǐn shí
若饮食

bù rú rén
不如人

wù shēng qī
勿生戚

【Poetic English Version】

Wearing and clothing,
eating and drinking,
not good enough?
Do not bluff.

【Interpretative English Version】 If your costume, food and drink look inferior, never groan.

wén guò nù
闻过怒

wén yù lè
闻誉乐

sǔn yǒu lái
损友来

yì yǒu què
益友却

【 Poetic English Version 】

Angry about demerits;
happy with plaudits.
Bad friends come.
Good friends numb.

【 Interpretative English Version 】 Never be overjoyed by others' praise of your contribution. Never fret about criticism. Otherwise, the bad will come your way, and the good will go away.

wén yù kǒng
闻誉恐

wén guò xīn
闻过欣

zhí liàng shì
直谅士

jiàn xiāng qīn
渐相亲

【 Poetic English Version 】

Afraid of plaudits,
pleased with demerits.
An upright chum
will close come.

【 Interpretative English Version 】 If you are uneasy with compliments, and comfortable with criticism, frank and virtuous friends will draw near to you.

wú xīn fēi
无心非

míng wéi cuò
名为错

yǒu xīn fēi
有心非

míng wéi è
名为恶

【 Poetic English Version 】

Wrong by accident,
only a mistake.
Wrong and negligent,
an evil sake.

【 Interpretative English Version 】 Doing something wrong by accident is only a mistake while doing something wrong by design is an evil.

guò néng gǎi
过能改

guī yú wú
归于无

tǎng yǎn shì
倘掩饰

zēng yì gū
增一辜

【 Poetic English Version 】

Faults being handled,
you're not befuddled.
Defects being concealed,
demerits are doubled.

【 Interpretative English Version 】 Correct your faults, and you will be clean and not confused. Cover them up, and your evil will be worsened.

dì wǔ zhāng fàn ài zhòng
第五章 泛爱众

Chapter 5 Love Every Being

The Planet and the Dragonfly

Written by Ray Murphy

A raging sphere grows elements to feed
The means from which all known life must breed
A dragonfly hovers for just one day
Man holds for earth, the key, to longer stay

地球与蜻蜓

瑞蒙·莫菲　作

许景城　译

天地狂，万物生，

众生昌，自然成。

蜻蜓绕，独一日，

持世钥，人长栖。

fán shì rén
凡是人

jiē xū ài
皆须爱

tiān tóng fù
天同覆

dì tóng zài
地同载

【Poetic English Version】

Man in feeling
love every being.
Same Heaven share;
same Earth bear.

【Interpretative English Version】 Love all creatures despite race and species, for they all dwell on the Earth and under the same sky.

xìng gāo zhě
行高者

míng zì gāo
名自高

rén suǒ zhòng
人所重

fēi mào gāo
非貌高

【Poetic English Version】

The better demeanor,
the more grace.
What we honor,
not nice face.

【Interpretative English Version】 Benign demeanors bring you respect and reputation. What people honor is your good behaviour not your good-looking countenance.

cái dà zhě
才大者

wàng zì dà
望自大

rén suǒ fú
人所服

fēi yán dà
非言大

【Poetic English Version】

Higher gifts fire,
further goes fame.
What we admire,
not bragging game!

【Interpretative English Version】 Great talent and wisdom engender great fame and prestige. What people admire is your great wisdom not your bragging.

jǐ yǒu néng
己有能

wù zì sī
勿自私

rén suǒ néng
人所能

wù qīng zǐ
勿轻訾

【Poetic English Version】

Good in talent,
selfless in domain.
Do not distain
those being competent.

【Interpretative English Version】 Never be selfish and please be selfless to society with your talents and abilities. Never distain and defame those with greater competence.

wù chǎn fù
勿谄富

wù jiāo pín
勿骄贫

wù yàn gù
勿厌故

wù xǐ xīn
勿喜新

【Poetic English Version】

Never bootlick gold,
nor poverty eschew.
Never distain th' old,
nor spoil th' new.

【Interpretative English Version】 Never flatter the rich or scorn the poor. Never desert the old, nor overindulge the new.

rén bù xián
人不闲

wù shì jiǎo
勿事搅

rén bù ān
人不安

wù huà rǎo
勿话扰

【Poetic English Version】

Do not disturb
those in busyness.
Do not perturb
those in distress.

【Interpretative English Version】 Never with trivial matters should you disturb others who are busy. Never with words should you bother others who are upset.

rén yǒu duǎn
人有短

qiè mò jiē
切莫揭

rén yǒu sī
人有私

qiè mò shuō
切莫说

【 Poetic English Version 】

Do not uncover
one's small defects.
Do not utter
one's private aspects.

【 Interpretative English Version 】 Never uncover others' shortcomings. Never divulge others' privacy.

dào rén shàn
道人善

jí shì shàn
即是善

rén zhī zhī
人知之

yù sī miǎn
愈思勉

【Poetic English Version】

Praising one's goodness
a real kindness.
Ones getting praise
better their ways.

【Interpretative English Version】Eulogizing others for their kindness is a real kindness. If others are praised, they will work harder and think about ways to better their behaviours and kindness.

yáng rén è
扬人恶

jí shì è
即是恶

jí zhī shèn
疾之甚

huò qiě zuò
祸且作

【Poetic English Version】

Spreading one's faults,
a real vice.
Too harsh assaults,
pay your price.

【Interpretative English Version】 Spreading others' demerits is indeed a demerit in the sense that too harsh and much criticism will brew hatred and troubles to you, and even cause upheavals.

shàn xiāng quàn
善相劝

dé jiē jiàn
德皆建

guò bù guī
过不规

dào liǎng kuī
道两亏

【Poetic English Version】

Goodness in urge,
virtues will emerge.
Faults not cured,
vice is endured.

【Interpretative English Version】 If goodness is mutually encouraged, you and your friends will both build up virtues. If faults fail to be mutually corrected, you both will worsen evil.

fán qǔ yǔ
凡取与

guì fēn xiǎo
贵分晓

yǔ yí duō
与宜多

qǔ yí shǎo
取宜少

【 Poetic English Version 】

Giving or taking,
that's a question?
Give more possession;
take less gaining.

【 Interpretative English Version 】 To give or to take, that's not a question. You'd better give more and take less.

jiāng jiā rén
将加人

xiān wèn jǐ
先问己

jǐ bù yù
己不欲

jí sù yǐ
即速已

【 Poetic English Version 】

Before forcing others,
weigh yourself first.
Hating being coerced,
stop forcing others.

【 Interpretative English Version 】 Never coerce others unless you ask yourself first whether or not you're willing to do it. If you're reluctant, it is better not to pressurize others.

ēn yù bào
恩欲报

yuàn yù wàng
怨欲忘

bào yuàn duǎn
报怨短

bào ēn cháng
报恩长

【Poetic English Version】

Repay one's kindness;
forget one's coldness.
Lessen bad attitudes;
deepen kind gratitudes.

【Interpretative English Version】 Repay others' kindness, and forget their coldness. Shorten your complaint and resentment, and prolong your repayment and deepen gratitudes to those in support of you.

dài bì pú
待婢仆

shēn guì duān
身贵端

suī guì duān
虽贵端

cí ér kuān
慈而宽

【 Poetic English Version 】

Treat servants well!
Noble you dwell!
Upright in mind,
always be kind.

【 Interpretative English Version 】 Treat your servants not only rightly and honourably, but also kindly and leniently. Set a good example for them to follow and show kindness and lenience to tell them what to do and how to improve their service.

shì fú rén
势服人

xīn bù rán
心不然

lǐ fú rén
理服人

fāng wú yán
方无言

【Poetic English Version】

Your power sown,
all will moan.
Your reason shown,
none will groan.

【Interpretative English Version】 Never win over others' hearts by force and rank, but by sense and sensibility.

dì liù zhāng qīn ài rén
第六章 亲爱仁

Chapter 6 Adhere to Virtues

Transience

A momentary pause in time

Written by Ray Murphy

Who can halt the relentless course of time?
Which moon decides the length of hour or day?
Can mortal whose construct it is, gainsay?
Measuring time is mere delusion.

稍纵即逝：昙花一现

瑞蒙·莫菲 作

许景城 译

光阴箭，孰能挡？

时日长，孰月管？

常人举，挽狂澜？

岁月旅，妄想量！

tóng shì rén
同是人

lèi bù qí
类不齐

liú sú zhòng
流俗众

rén zhě xī
仁者希

【Poetic English Version】

Man on Earth,
varies in race.
Average in place.
Virtues in dearth.

【Interpretative English Version】 Humanity under heaven vary in race, nationality and class. The majority are average minds while few are great minds of virtue.

guǒ rén zhě
果仁者

rén duō wèi
人多畏

yán bú huì
言不讳

sè bú mèi
色不媚

【Poetic English Version】

Good great Muse,
we often revere:
talk no taboos;
allow no jeer.

【Interpretative English Version】 Great minds are often revered for the reason that they are sincerely unafraid to tell truth. They are upright and not fawning.

néng qīn rén
能亲仁

wú xiàn hǎo
无限好

dé rì jìn
德日进

guò rì shǎo
过日少

【Poetic English Version】

Adhere to benevolence;
maintain endless reverence.
Virtues daily gain;
faults daily wane.

【Interpretative English Version】 Adhering to those of great virtue and goodness engenders infinite benefits. If you are consistent, your virtues will increase daily and your flaws will daily decrease.

bù qīn rén
不亲仁

wú xiàn hài
无限害

xiǎo rén jìn
小人进

bǎi shì huài
百事坏

【Poetic English Version】

Fail to adhere,
endless harms incur.
Bad minds come,
all turn dumb.

【Interpretative English Version】 Failing to adhere to those of great virtues and goodness provokes infinite detriments. By doing so, small minds will come along and your reputation will be tarnished.

dì qī zhāng　yú lì xué wén
第七章　余力学文

Chapter 7　Learn Arts as Gift Starts

The Dancer

Written by Ray Murphy

The Dancer moves in poise and grace, with ease,
She steps light on the floor to tell a tale,
Of cultures drawing near to understand,
Ever, the Arts will conquer divided land.

舞　者

瑞蒙·莫菲　作

许景城　译

雅姿舞，步轻盈，

蹈悠扬，叙事兴，

文化繁，趋同解，

艺文聚，分地合。

bù lì xíng
不力行

dàn xué wén
但学文

zhǎng fú huá
长浮华

chéng hé rén
成何人

【Poetic English Version】

Practice no goodness,
learn just art,
comes more glibness!
You show part!

【Interpretative English Version】 If you fail to practice all those virtues mentioned previously but simply commit to further learning, you are only superficial and become useless in practice.

dàn lì xíng
但力行

bù xué wén
不学文

rèn jǐ jiàn
任己见

mèi lǐ zhēn
昧理真

【 **Poetic English Version** 】

Practice goodness right,
learn no art,
shallow your insight,
truth comes apart!

【 **Interpretative English Version** 】 Stubbornness and fatuousness will result if you only know the practice of virtues but without further learning.

dú shū fǎ
读书法

yǒu sān dào
有三到

xīn yǎn kǒu
心眼口

xìn jiē yào
信皆要

【Poetic English Version】

What learning requires?
Three things heeded:
Heart, mouth, eyes.
Faith also needed.

【Interpretative English Version】 When studying, make sure your heart, your eyes, and your mouth are engaged. Faith, honesty and confidence are equally important.

fāng dú cǐ
方读此

wù mù bǐ
勿慕彼

cǐ wèi zhōng
此未终

bǐ wù qǐ
彼勿起

【Poetic English Version】

Reading this one,
never admire that.
This not done,
never start that.

【Interpretative English Version】 When reading this book, never be absent-minded, nor admire reading the other. Never pick up another book until this one is finished.

kuān wéi xiàn
宽为限

jǐn yòng gōng
紧用功

gōng fu dào
工夫到

zhì sè tōng
滞塞通

【Poetic English Version】

Loose plans laid,
hard work made.
Enough efforts paid,
doubts will fade.

【Interpretative English Version】 If you set a loose study plan, your minds will get relaxation that enables you to study harder, broaden your vision and reach your goal. Once you make enough efforts, problems and troubles will be dissolved with acquired knowledge and experience.

xīn yǒu yí
心有疑

suí zhá jì
随札记

jiù rén wèn
就人问

qiú què yì
求确义

【Poetic English Version】

Questions in mind,
please note down.
Ask and find,
clear answers grown.

【Interpretative English Version】 Note down what confuses you and either ask someone for explanations or search for relevant information to help dispel your doubts.

fáng shì qīng
房室清

qiáng bì jìng
墙壁净

jī àn jié
几案洁

bǐ yàn zhèng
笔砚正

【Poetic English Version】

Keep rooms clean,
walls tidy scene.
Keep desks uncluttered,
brushes 'n inkstones ordered.

【Interpretative English Version】 Keep your room clean and walls tidy. Keep your desk uncluttered and your stationery items orderly.

mò mó piān
墨磨偏

xīn bù duān
心不端

zì bú jìng
字不敬

xīn xiān bìng
心先病

【 Poetic English Version 】

Inkstones looking messy
indicates minds galled/go.
Words looking scrawled
suggests hearts uneasy.

【 Interpretative English Version 】 Your inkstone is messy, which results from your bewildered mind and will further leads to your sloppy writing.

liè diǎn jí
列典籍

yǒu dìng chù
有定处

dú kàn bì
读看毕

huán yuán chù
还原处

【Poetic English Version】

Sort books out
by proper heading.
Done the reading,
keep original layout.

【Interpretative English Version】 Classify your books in proper places and by heading. Return them to where they belong when you finish reading.

suī yǒu jí
虽有急

juàn shù qí
卷束齐

yǒu quē sǔn
有缺损*

jiù bǔ zhī
就补之

* 有版本为“有缺坏”。

【 Poetic English Version 】

Despite your rush,
stash books tight.
If books crush,
repair them right.

【 Interpretative English Version 】 Though in a hurry, roll up your books neatly. Repair any missing or damaged pages promptly.

fēi shèng shū
非圣书

bǐng wù shì
屏勿视

bì cōng míng
蔽聪明

huài xīn zhì
坏心志

【Poetic English Version】

If books dirty,
be never thumbed.
Smother your genius,
or wills numbed.

【Interpretative English Version】 Never touch any text that might corrupt your soul, such as books and videos associated with superstition, violence, drugs or pornography. If you touch them, your intelligence and aspirations will be ruined.

wù zì bào
勿自暴

wù zì qì
勿自弃

shèng yǔ xián
圣与贤

kě xùn zhì
可驯致

【Poetic English Version】

Curb your rage.
Yield no nature.
Virtue and sage,
better your nurture.

【Interpretative English Version】 Never disdain yourself. Nor give up. Please believe: to be a sage or a person of virtue, you can be gradually trained and cultivated.

Initial English Translation： 21/04/2012—22/06/2013

Revised English Translation： 15/04/2016—05/05/2016

Finalized English Translation: 01/10/2019—28/10/2019

Illustration: 16/04/2016—05/09/2017

"Two Dragons" in Dialogue

Dr David Joyner

(Confucius Institute, Bangor University, Wales, UK)

Dizigui (*Standards for Disciples*) is one of the most important canonical works of Chinese culture. Written between the seventeenth and eighteenth centuries AD, this ancient text, which interprets some of the fundamental principles and practices of Confucius's writing of more than two millennia earlier, has been prized and revered by Chinese people, high and low, up to the present day. It is therefore a valuable insight for non-Chinese, a **sine qua non** for people from Western and other countries into the Chinese psyche, and to some extent into their motivations, beliefs, societal structure and ways of behaving in various situations.

Western people often misinterpret modern China and the Chinese as they imagine that their strong engagement in global economics, cultural exchange, business investment and increasing activity in geopolitics represents a "Westernization" of China and dilution of the influence of its ancient and distinct cultural background. Whilst no doubt many Chinese that travel abroad, especially for education, do add to their own cultural background some of the richness of other cultures, even in the second largest world economy there is still a strong influence of the principles passed down through the ages from the ancient sages, through Confucius and then through several key text such as the present *Dizigui*. Thus, whilst many of the strict societal practices and structures were swept aside in the West following the Second World War, China has largely retained its respect for the ancient ways and there is still more emphasis on duties and responsibility than on rights, by contrast with the Western tendency.

In this context, this work by Peter Jingcheng Xu is to be warmly welcomed as it makes this important *Dizigui* text accessible to English language speakers. Not only has Xu taken considerable pains to translate and interpret the ancient three-character poetry with a prose translation in clear attractive language, avoiding archaisms and clumsiness which is off-putting to modern readers; but he has also provided a poetic version which combines clarity of meaning with a satisfying flow of English rhyme and rhythm. Some earlier versions of this work suffer from archaisms, which detract from its appeal.

I think that this excellent new work is invaluable for Chinese and non-Chinese alike:

For foreign students and casual observers of China, it is useful because it explains many of the traditional instructions to disciples, which she/he can calibrate against behaviour that they observe today. Also, the verses can be easily learnt and recited or set to music, and they can be used to teach the language as Chinese culture and practice will be appreciated whilst the characters are taught. As each line is only three characters long, this makes for a highly "digestible" offering. This is an important aspect of maintaining motivation and fostering a sense of achievement for the intrepid student of a culture which is very unfamiliar to most Westerners and a language which is recognized to be one of the most difficult to master.

For Chinese people, as the English versions are carefully designed for Western ways of expression and understanding, these can show them how they can explain their practices and the thinking behind them in ways that can be easily appreciated by non-Chinese.

As the Director of the Confucius Institute at Bangor University, I have the privilege of trying to understand this ancient and complex culture and of working to promote the exchange of cultures between Wales and China through our approach of emphasizing "Two Dragons" — two voices in conversation, two equal cultures striving to understand the other and to explain their own. This work, which presents also a careful translation into English (one of the two nativè languages in this country, alongside the ancient but thriving Welsh language) in poetry and prose, provides a vauable insight into the basis of China's rich heritage and its valuable contribution to mankind's story. To native Welsh speakers and learners, the Chinese culture is directly accessible through one of the most important canonical texts. Peter Jingcheng Xu is one of a new generation of interpreters of Chinese culture whose efforts, we hope and trust, will continue for many decades to make many more of these canonical works of the Chinese heritage available in attractive, flowing text and prose.

Speaking personally, I see the intellectual and emotional journey to learning about China as rambling across a huge highland massif. As I mount one summit, with a grateful sigh and a feeling of satisfaction, another higher one emerges from the mist. As I lift my eyes, I see that the peaks stretch on and on to a distant horizon. I often wonder that I am surprised by this, given that the country has over four millennia of recorded history during most of which it has been one of the major world cultures and a dominant power. The socio-economic background to this major portion of the global population is so different from our own that it demands intense study and a nuanced understanding. It repays the effort but always challenges us to search out more truths. This present work is just the sort of material we need as life-long students. I am delighted to welcome it as an important new resource, making my learning a pleasure and encouraging me to ramble through some of the most important cultural landscapes of ancient prodigy but modern relevance.

Bangor, Wales

27/04/2016

An Eco–Impressionist Way of Illustrating *Dizigui*

Ray Murphy

(Confucius Institute, Bangor University, Wales, UK)

When Peter Jingcheng Xu approached me to provide some illustrations for his work on the *Dizigui*, he was in fact calling in a card. In the past he had translated some of my poetry into Chinese alongside images that I had created, which added value and a new dimension to my work. I therefore undertook his request in gratitude for this but with mounting trepidation because the source material did not readily lend itself to straight portrayal in visual terms.

Peter Jingcheng Xu is a gifted translator, poet, and academic. Whereas I am but an artist and sometimes poet. In reality, I am a painter of land and seascapes employing visual tricks and devices to create atmosphere in what I portray. I am also a printmaker. The first question was, how I could turn these skills to illustrating what essentially to me is a philosophical treatise on human behaviour. I wanted on all counts to avoid creating a series of cartoon like images in progressively similar format. If asked, I describe that I am an "Impressionist" in style. I also subscribe to the view of the romantics that painting, poetry and music are inextricably linked. I therefore wanted to provide something beyond the simple image adding quatrains of my own poetry to emphasise the link to Peter Jingcheng Xu's interpretation of the *Dizigui*.

A good place to start was to actually read the *Dizigui* and Xu's interpretation. I cannot claim to have liked everything I read in the *Dizigui* which I found outmoded in part. Peter Jingcheng Xu, however, had given me a free hand and I needed to approach the work creatively. I would deliver a set of work in various media and it is then up to who commissioned the work to accept or reject what is offered. My only stipulation was that I was not subject to censorship. I also took the advice that what was originally written over three hundred years has been amended for modern life by those in China impressed by its core values.

I started by focusing on certain words that I associated

with human quality. I narrowed them down to seven to mirror the number of chapters in Xu's work. I then undertook to provide seven illustrations in various media. In the end, I produced a number of paintings and woodcut prints.

The creative process was thus kickstarted. The seven words chosen were, honest, virtuous, incorruptible, trustworthy, ethical, principled and creative. At that point, I obtained the Chinese calligraphy for each of them in the ancient seal script. This was in a rather forlorn hope that I could use them in some way if I ventured into work of the abstract. So through a period of trial, error and rejection, I worked until I realised that I would have to think of an overall subject matter that I could fit my visual and written work into. The answer was provided indirectly by Peter Jingcheng Xu who described his doctoral research as "Anthropocenic ecopoetics". After I had looked up what this meant, I understood I could centre my illustrations and poetry on matters of ecological concern as well as the human values that affected them.

I wrote the quatrain pieces of poetry to emphasise the

subject matter of the paintings and prints. In addition, this created a link for me to the original format of the *Dizigui*. In simple terms, they relate to the relationship between human beings and further on the possible destruction of the planet they inhabit. This is a particular focus on the human virtues and duty needed to secure the Earth's future. I have produced work that encompasses painting, Intaglio prints and woodcut prints. In joining this media together, I am happy that my illustrations and poetry are resonant with what Peter Jingcheng Xu has written in the first part of the introduction in his valuable contribution to the understanding of the *Dizigui*.

Bangor, Wales

12/12/2017

Words from the Translator

Dr Peter Jingcheng Xu

(Guangdong University of Foreign Studies, China; Bangor University, Wales, UK)

Admittedly, this book has taken me a long time to translate, revise, and accomplish, and many people and institutions have undoubtedly offered helps in varied ways. First and foremost, my sincere gratitude goes to Guangdong University of Foreign Studies, Bangor University, and Beijing Forestry University for their generous and wholehearted supports for this project.

I am very fortunate to have Dr David Joyner, Ex Foreign Director of the Confucius Institute, Bangor University to scrupulously proofread my English renderings, write an afterword, and endorse the free-of-charge and eternal use of the CI logo of "Twin Dragons" in my works. As expressing my debt of thanks for his unflagging support,

I must add that all the final accountability for the renderings of course rest entirely with myself and I am alone to be required to account for omissions, errors and mistakes. I am deeply indebted to Mr Ray Murphy, artist in residence of the Confucius Institute for his passion and endorsement by painting the illustrations for this book, whose exotic perspectives and techniques I believe without doubt will make it more attractive to readers.

Special gratitude goes to Professor Scott Slovic, Chair of the Department of English of the University of Idaho, and the founding president of the Association for the Study of Literature and Environment (ASLE) and editor of the journal *ISLE: Interdisciplinary Studies in Literature and Environment* for composing an insightful preface titled "An Eco-Confucian Instruction Manual for Good Behaviour" which explores the unexpected affinities between Chinese Confucian *Dizigui* and some key Western environmental literatures, or in his words, "jeremiadic and rhapsodic texts", in terms of informing and guiding humanity towards right behaviours that are urgently needed in the age of Anthropocene. I also express my sincerest thanks to Dr Christopher Schliephake, a cultural historian and ecocritic from University of Augsburg for his preface that is broad enough to situate *Dizigui* within a transcultural poetic framework. Furthermore, particular thanks go to Emeritus Professor Ian Gregson from the School of English Literature, Bangor University for his preface that professionally curates the literary and cultural exchanges between this Confucian primer and environmental Western campaigners' works. I also would like to thank Professor Zhonglian Huang from Guangdong University of Foreign Studies for his endorsement that hails the values of this book through the prism of Translation Studies.

Many constructive suggestions from Dr Andrew Webb, Dean of the School of English Literature (now the School of Languages, Literatures and Linguistics), Bangor University, Professor Helen Wilcox, ex-Dean of the same school, and Dr Samuel Rogers, an academic sibling, currently senior lecturer in English Literature at University of the West of England, Bristol, to whom I am deeply grateful, make this a much better book than it was initially. My dear friend Feng Wang, a PhD degree achiever in Translation Studies from Tongji University, Shanghai, and a researcher in Jilin University, also deserves my thanks for offering some advice in terms of multimodal promotion among Chinese scholars and students.

Prior to publication, I have tested the applicability of these guidelines in this book by teaching certain principles to a range of local students, from primary schools to those in Bangor University, or by asking my friends to read the earlier drafts and comment how they and the local students react to these principles in English. For this reason, I am deeply indebted to Dr Jianmin Fang, Vice Principal of the North Wales Chinese School and her faculties, such as Ms Kun Jiao, for their great support and permission for me to have those investigations into the British-born Chinese children. Based on their feedback and taking into consideration target-language users' reading habits and aesthetics, I have revised the renderings to the extent of balancing the faithfulness to the source-language textual meanings and the readability so as to enhance the accessibility and acceptability by Western readers. Thanks should also be given to Mr Alan Edwards, Director of

Bangor University International Students Support Service, and his colleagues Ms Melanie Brown, Ms Katerina Videnskaya, and Ms Karen Mai Jones for their passionate interest in this programme; to my friends in Bangor, such as Mr Stephen Rowlands, Mr Cecil Condron, Dr Joanna Melville-richards, Ms Leah Lloyd Stanton, Ms Vivienne Pritchard, Ms Mina Park, Ms Sarah Grawe, Mr Will Stewart, Ms Eabhan Ni Shuileabhain, Ms Darina Angelova, Ms Martina Angelova, Ms Elizabeth Vipond, Mr Robert James Blyth, and Mr Jonathan Perons for their passionate advice; to the staff team of the Confucius Institute, Bangor University like Professor Liying Zhang, Associate Professor Tao Zeng, Professor Yanjun Xin, Associate Professor Kunyan Li, Dr Lina Davitt, Ms Vicky Washington, Dr Fengxian Yang, Professor Huayi Liu, Mr Mengnan Shi, Ms Yuan Liu, Ms Xuan Yu, and Mr Junming Huo for their teaching and promoting my English translations and Chinese guidelines in the local schools; to my PhD and MA colleagues in Bangor University, such as Dr Euidon Donny Joo, Dr Dhaifallah Alotaibi, Dr Syed Ajijur Rahman, Dr Jaber Saleh Alsufyani, Dr Ammar Alabassi, Dr Daniel

Hughes, Dr Anna Luepke, Dr Sven Greitschus, Dr Ping Zhang, Dr Changjing Liu, Dr Jinquan Yu, Dr Chunli Shen, Dr Shizhe Wang, Mr Ming Wei, Dr Shuge Zhang, Dr Yan Ma, Mr Zhen Fu, Ms Ting Wang, Mr Zhizhuo Li, Mr Fei Li, Ms Shanshan Lu, Ms Qinrui Zhang, Mr Yixuan Qian, Mr Zhiwen Zhou, Miss Kate Rongkai Hu, Mr Jingsheng Hu, Mr Sishan Hu, and Ms Dan Li; and to the visiting scholars such as Professor Jinxue Fan, Associate Professor Lin Shen, Dr Xian Zhao, Dr Zhizhou Kong, Dr Yuying Shi, Associate Professor Lizhong Sun, Dr Shan Gao, Ms Xiaoling Wang, Mr Tong Xie, Professor Yalian Zhang, Professor Dong Li, Ms Hui Lu, Professor Yangquan Li, Professor Hui Chen, Associate Professor Yujuan Feng, Ms Tingting Qiu, Associate Professor Weifeng Xin, Professor Jiehui Hu, Professor Lihua Yang, Dr Chunling Tang, Associate Professor Shangmin Lü, Dr Anbang Wang, Dr Bingjie Wang, Ms Hong Hu, Associate Professor Yi Teng, Dr Hongyu Zeng, Associate Professor Yanhua Li, Dr Yingrong Chen, Professor Chunlei Jiang and Ms Fang Li for their sincere advice based on their diverse professions.

My greatest gratitude also goes to the teachers and

friends of my alma mater, Beijing Forestry University that enlightened my expertise, career and way, and offered kind supports, such as Professor Baohui Shi, Professor Meifang Nangong, Mrs Bronwyn Jane Anzai, Professor Keqin Duan, Professor Jiangmei Wu, Professor Wenke Xiao, Professor Rongping Cao, Professor Tiezheng Li, Professor Ying Zi, Professor Guowen Zhou, Professor Li Fan, Professor Jian Li, Professor Xiaoyu Huang, Associate Professor Zhi Li, Associate Professor Lihong Wu, Associate Professor Hongmei Zhu, Associate Professor Jing Su, Associate Professor Qing Chang, Associate Professor Kui Zhu, Associate Professor Tingting Fan, Associate Professor Lisha Chen, Associate Professor Jiawei Tao, Associate Professor Yueqin Gao, Associate Professor Bing Li, Associate Professor Guoxia Zu, Associate Professor Xin Li, Associate Professor Wei Liu, Associate Professor Xiaoying Chen, Associate Professor Lita Lü, Associate Professor Can Luo, Associate Professor Hailong Yang, Dr Tao Zheng, Mr Qi Dai, Ms Dan Yang, Ms Yanxi Qin, Ms Xiaoni Tan, Ms Yudan Jiang, Ms Juan Huang, Ms Cuiqiong Liu, Mr Xiangbin Kong, Mr Ruiguang Liu, Mr Yu Chen, Ms Linlin

Han, Dr Zhanzhan Lan, Ms Fan Wu, Ms Yu Xiang, Ms Qiongxian Wu, Ms Ying Li, Ms Jinli Zeng, Mr Wenche Yang, and Mr Li Wan.

In terms of publication, I also benefit enormously from the generosity of those who share funding resources information and a wide spectrum of irreplaceable suggestion, especially my colleagues and friends here in Guangdong University of Foreign Studies and other institutes in Guangzhou such as Professor Yan Liu, Professor Xin Zhang, Professor Jinwei Dong, Professor Zhuang Wu, Professor Humin Liu, Mr Shaoxiong Lin, Associate Professor Rui Han, Ms Xiaomei Huang, Professor Chengtuan Li, Professor Maosheng Liu, Professor Weisheng Tang, Professor Ming Li, Professor Yuanhua Xie, Pofessor Xiaowei He, Professor Huhua Ouyang, Professor Yuan Li, Professor Jing Yang, Professor Xiaoqing Qiu, Professor Min Jiao, Associate Professor Jinjin Fu, Associate Professor Xiaoyan Cai, Associate Professor Dongqing Wang, Associate Professor Zhuyu Jiang, Ms Yukun Xia, Dr Yunfeng Wang, Dr Wei Feng, Dr Feng Ding, Dr Qiuming Lin, Associate Professor Qunying Huang, Dr Zirong Li, Mr

Licheng Lu, Dr Zhe Chen, Professor Xudong Wu, Professor Yinong Zhao, Ms Chunmei Pan, Associate Professor Manzhen Yang, Ms Li Yang, Dr Tie Zheng, Associate Professor Jianming Guan, Professor Haonong Pang, Ms Yujie Xie, Ms Lan Guo, Ms Lan Zhang, Associate Professor Mianjun Xu, Associate Propessor Jing Shi, Professor Li Yang, Ms Leling Li, Mr Yunnan Hou, Ms Hong Yang, Dr Yiting Qiu, Mr Xiao Ma, Mr Dong Wang, Ms Shujun Chen, Mr Changqing Zheng, Ms Xi Wang, Ms Xiaole Shi, Ms Zidan Li, Ms Yuming Chen, Ms Baoyu Fu, Dr Ming Quan, Miss Xiaocong Liang, Miss Yishuang Zheng, Dr Zhanping Wang, Professor Chengsheng Jiang, and Mr Shijun Zhao; no less significantly also from the friends working in a variety of key presses in China, such as Mr Junjun Jiang, a professional editor from Shanghai Foreign Language Education Press, and Ms Ying Yang, a public-spirited editor from Science Press, Beijing. To all of them, my reverence is given. I also want to express the deepest appreciation to Ms Jingjing Chen, a passionate, adept and responsible editor from Intellectual Property Publishing House, without whose patient assistance, this entire book would remain obscure in my computer disk otherwise.

Last but not least, I owe the deepest debt to my family and relatives for their consistent support, love and understanding of my little time to return my care and love while I was deciphering this enlightening Confucian text.

To end this epilogue, I would like to quote a poem written by myself:

Soldiering On

Looking back, I find, I've come a long way;
of wonders in the sea, still I won't stray.
Looking up at the stars, I know quite well,
in Earth's gutter and plot, we all flitter,
as meteors in flashing tails glitter.
Looking forward, as the nymphs' wings flutter,
as if a new life's showing, I utter:
For health, home and happiness tolls the bell.

Initially written at Menai View Terrace, Bangor
23/04/2016 – 03/12/2017
Revised by White Clouds Mountain, Guangzhou
01/10/2019—15/11/2019